U.S. Fish & Wildlife Service

# Annual Report of Lands Under Control of the U.S. Fish & Wildlife Service

*as of September 30, 2006*

# Annual Report of Lands Under Control Of the U.S. Fish and Wildlife Service As of September 30, 2006

*Compiled by: Division of Realty*

# Message from the Director

We've come a long way since 1903, when the National Wildlife Refuge System began when one man, Paul Kroegel—equipped with a badge, a gun, a boat, and lots of determination—watched over Florida's Pelican Island. The once-idealistic notion that we should set aside and protect land for intrinsically valuable wildlife is now a reality. Today, our 547 refuges encompass more than 96 million acres that support a rich variety of wildlife, including more than 280 endangered or threatened species. National wildlife refuges—as well as waterfowl production areas and coordination areas—are consistent and visible reflections of the federal government's pledge to its citizens that there will always be lands and waters where plants and animals can thrive.

With more than 71 percent of the land in the United States held in private ownership, the well-being and continued diversity of America's wildlife depends on the active involvement of conservation-minded private citizens. Conservation is not a spectator sport. It takes the combined commitment of federal and state agencies, conservation organizations, local communities, and many other stakeholders to ensure that our natural resources will be preserved and protected today and for generations to come.

Our partners continued to step forward in Fiscal Year 2006. Consider the largest single land purchase by the Service in the fiscal year—2,833 acres acquired for $3.4 million for the San Bernard National Wildlife Refuge in a rapidly developing area south of Houston. This crucial addition was made possible with the cooperation of the National Fish and Wildlife Foundation.

Some 6,270 acres of seasonally flooded bottomland in one of the most important and vulnerable wetland areas of the Mississippi River Delta were made a part of the Catahoula National Wildlife Refuge in Louisiana, through a partnership composed of Wal-Mart's "Acres for America" program, The Conservation Fund, American Electric Power, the National Fish and Wildlife Foundation, and the Service. These lands will play an important role in the Service's carbon sequestration efforts.

In Minnesota, the Service acquired 1,241 acres of conservation easements and 16 acres in fee ownership at the Northern Tallgrass Prairie National Wildlife Refuge. Funding from the Legislative Committee for Minnesota Resources has helped clear the way for the acquisition of several more key fee and easement tracts. Partners such as the Brandenburg Prairie Foundation and The Nature Conservancy have also supported our acquisition and protection efforts in the state.

In Montana, the Service established the Rocky Mountain Front Conservation Area by purchasing the first conservation easement, covering 4,177 acres worth $1,535,000. The Service contributed $1 million, The Nature Conservancy donated $100,000, and the landowner contributed the remaining $435,000 in value. TNC's Montana Chapter was awarded the Service's annual National Land Protection Award for significant contributions to land-protection partnerships with the Service.

National wildlife refuges are places where high-quality, safe, and enjoyable wildlife-dependent recreation connects visitors to their natural resource heritage. More than 39 million visitors each year find the mountains, valleys, deserts, meadows and wetlands of national wildlife refuges to be some of the most scenic places in America. As our Nation becomes more urbanized and Americans become more disassociated from our outdoor heritage, national wildlife refuges are vital links with nature for most American families. There is a national wildlife refuge within 50 miles of most major cities, giving families a close-to-home place to see firsthand how important natural resource conservation is in our daily lives.

National wildlife refuges are places of solitude and serenity amid the noise and bustle of urban and suburban life. They are places where a youngster can learn to cast a fishing line or recognize a bird they have just come to know. They are places where families can reinforce their own relationships, one generation passing to the next recollections of days spent listening to a bullfrog or watching butterflies pollinate flower after flower.

National wildlife refuges do more than welcome those who want to hunt, fish, or just watch wildlife. They also teach Americans to become conservation constituents by fostering understanding of the central role of wildlife and wildlife habitat in our daily lives and our nation's traditions.

For all the dedication of our hard-working staff professionals, we could neither operate nor maintain our magnificent habitats without the assistance of volunteers. During Fiscal Year 2006, close to 34,000 volunteers donated more than 1.3 million hours to the Service on behalf of wildlife conservation. Those hours represent the equivalent of more than $23 million. Our volunteers are not shy about getting their hands dirty; the largest number of volunteer hours—more than 437,000—were invested in wildlife and habitat work. In addition, more than 200 nonprofit Refuge Friends organizations bring a special dimension of citizen service to the Fish and Wildlife Service. Their support is critical to fulfilling our conservation mission.

In this era of intense development, it is ever more important that we continue to protect critical habitat to ensure the health of the nation's fish, wildlife, and plant resources. In support of this mission, Service Realty Offices completed 473 transactions in Fiscal Year 2006.

In community after community, national wildlife refuges give people a firsthand chance to appreciate fish and wildlife ecology and understand their role in the environment. The challenge today is to engage all segments of the American public in a dialogue about the contributions of wildlife to a healthy human environment. All of us can take great pride in our part in those efforts.

H. Dale Hall

Director

# KEY TO REAL PROPERTY NUMBERS

## SEPTEMBER 30, 2006

| No. | Property |
|---|---|
| 3 | Neosho NFH, MO |
| 5 | Leadville NFH, CO |
| 6 | Craig Brook NFH, ME |
| 11 | Bozeman Fish Technology Cen., MT |
| 14 | Erwin NFH, TN |
| 15 | Nashua NFH, NH |
| 17 | D. C. Booth NFH, SD |
| 18 | Warm Springs NFH, GA |
| 19 | Edenton NFH, NC |
| 22 | White Sulphur Springs NFH, WV |
| 23 | Private John Allen NFH, MS |
| 25 | Pelican Island NWR, FL |
| 26 | Mammoth Spring NFH, AR |
| 27 | Bretton NWR, LA |
| 28 | Stump Lake NWR, ND |
| 29 | Wichita Mountains Wildlife Ref., OK |
| 30 | Huron NWR, MI |
| 31 | Passage Key NWR, FL |
| 32 | Shell Keys NWR, LA |
| 33 | Three Arch Rocks NWR, OR |
| 34 | Copalis NWR, WA |
| 35 | Flattery Rocks NWR, WA |
| 36 | Quillayute Needles NWR, WA |
| 38 | Key West NWR, FL |
| 39 | Lower Klamath NWR, CA & OR |
| 40 | Malheur NWR, OR |
| 41 | Chase Lake NWR, ND |
| 41-1 | Island Bay NWR, FL |
| 42 | Mille Lacs NWR, MN |
| 44 | Cold Spring NWR, OR |
| 46 | Deer Flat NWR, ID & OR |
| 47 | Minidoka NWR, ID |
| 52 | Culebra NWR, PR |
| 53 | Farallon NWR, CA |
| 58 | National Bison Range, MT |
| 58-1 | Pittsford NFH, VT |
| 60 | Quilene NWR, WA |
| 61 | Bear Lake NWR, CA |
| 63 | Fort Niobrara NWR, NE |
| 65 | Green Bay NWR, WI |
| 67 | Orangeburg NFH, SC |
| 69 | Gravel Island NWR, WI |
| 73 | Anaho Island NWR, NV |
| 74 | National Elk Refuge, WY |
| 75 | Saratoga NFH, WY |
| 77 | Dungeness NWR, WA |
| 78 | Mille Lacs NWR, MN |
| 79 | Big Lake NWR, AR |
| 81 | North Platte NWR, NE |
| 82 | Berkshire Trout Hatchery, MA |
| 85 | Nine-Pipe NWR, MT |
| 86 | Pablo NWR, MT |
| 88 | Sullys Hill Nat. Game Preserve, ND |
| 91 | Blackwood Island NWR, GA |
| 93 | Upper Mississippi River Wildlife & Fish Refuge, IL, MN, WI |
| 95 | Johnston Island NWR, (Pacific Area inset) |
| 98 | Santwich NWR, GA & SC |
| 100 | McKay Creek NWR, OR |
| 103 | Upper Klamath NWR, OR |
| 105 | Pathfinder NWR, WY |
| 108 | Fishermans NWR, OK |
| 109 | Tula Lake NWR, CA |
| 113 | Bear River Migratory Bird Ref., UT |
| 114 | Cedar Keys NWR, FL |
| 115 | Benton Lake NWR, MT |
| 117 | Salt Plains NWR, OK |
| 118 | Cape Romain NWR, SC |
| 119 | Wolf Island NWR, GA |
| 121 | Salton Sea NWR, CA |
| 122 | Sheldon NWR, NV & OR |
| 124 | St. Marks NWR, FL |
| 125 | Crescent Lake NWR, ME |
| 128 | Camas NFH, WI |
| 127 | Natchoches NFH, LA |
| 128 | Fallon NWR, WA |
| 129 | Hagerman NFH, ID |
| 131 | Ennis NFH, MT |
| 133 | Dexter NFH, NM |
| 135 | Lamar NFH, PA |
| 140 | Hudson Lake NWR, WY |
| 141 | Bamforth NWR, WY |
| 142 | Long Lake NWR, ND |
| 146 | Swanquarter NWR, NC |
| 148 | Blackwater NWR, MD |
| 159 | Harrison Lake NFH, VA |
| 160 | Mattamuskeet NWR, NC |
| 162 | Trempealeau NWR, WI |
| 164 | Des Lacs NWR, ND |
| 165 | J. Clark Salyer NWR, ND |
| 167 | Arrowwood NWR, ND |
| 168 | Sand Lake NWR, SD |
| 169 | Lacreek NWR, SD |
| 170 | Lostwood NWR, ND |
| 172 | Medicine Lake NWR, MT |
| 173 | Lake Andes NWR, SD |
| 174 | Canfield Lake NWR, ND |
| 175 | Chautauqua NWR, IL |
| 176 | Waubay NWR, SD |
| 177 | Red Rock Lakes NWR, MT |
| 178 | Oregon Islands NWR, OR |
| 179 | Lake Isom NWR, TN |
| 180 | Seney NWR, MI |
| 183 | Valentine NWR, NE |
| 184 | Uvalde NFH, TX |
| 185 | Upper Souris NWR, ND |
| 187 | White River NWR, AR |
| 188 | Hart Mtn. Nat. Antelope Refuge, OR |
| 191 | Muleshoe NWR, TX |
| 192 | Rice Lake NWR, MN |
| 193 | Delta NWR, LA |
| 194 | Tamarac NWR, MN |
| 195 | Bowdoin NWR, MT |
| 196 | Kellys Slough NWR, ND |
| 199 | Bitter Lake NWR, NM |
| 200 | Desert NWR, NV |
| 201 | Swan Lake NWR, MO |
| 202 | Storm Lake NWR, ND |
| 203 | Tewaukon NWR, ND |
| 206 | Ardoch NWR, ND |
| 207 | Turnbull NWR, WA |
| 210 | Willapa NWR, WA |
| 211 | Camas NWR, ID |
| 213 | Okefenokee NWR, FL & GA |
| 214 | Yazoo NWR, MS |
| 215 | Charles M. Russell NWR, MT |
| 217 | Patuxent Research Refuge, MD |
| 218 | Bosque del Apache NWR, NM |
| 220 | Moosehorn NWR, ME |
| 221 | Sacramento NWR, CA |
| 223 | Union Slough NWR, IA |
| 224 | Bombay Hook NWR, DE |
| 225 | Agassiz NWR, MN |
| 231 | Red Island NWR, NC |
| 232 | Bear Butte NWR, SD |
| 233 | Carson NFH, WA |
| 234 | Montezuma NWR, NY |
| 236 | Lake Thibodeau NWR, MT |
| 240 | Lacassine NWR, LA |
| 241 | Ruby Lake NWR, NV |
| 242 | Aransas NWR, TX |
| 245 | Sabine NWR, LA |
| 246-1 | McKinney Lake NFH, NC |
| 247 | Block Coulee NWR, WA |
| 248 | Back Bay NWR, VA |
| 249 | Hewitt Lake NWR, MT |
| 252 | Iroa Dam NWR, TX |
| 253 | Chattahoochee Forest NFH, GA |
| 254 | Corning NFH, AR |
| 255 | Tybee NWR, SC |
| 257 | Leavenworth NFH, WA |
| 259 | Valley City NFH, ND |
| 260 | Valley City NFH, ND |
| 262 | West Sister Island NWR, OH |
| 267 | Cape Meares NWR, OR |
| 268 | Crest White Heron NWR, FL |
| 268 | Mashto NFH, FL |
| 269 | Piedmont NWR, GA |
| 270 | Cabeza Prieta NWR, AZ |
| 271 | Kofa NWR, AZ |
| 272 | Meridian NFH, MS |
| 274 | Necedah NWR, WI |
| 275 | Carolina Sandhills NWR, SC |
| 278 | Williams Creek NFH, AZ |
| 281 | Little Pend Oreille NWR, WA |
| 285 | Buffalo Lake NWR, TX |
| 288 | Garfield Lake NWR, ND |
| 292 | Florence Lake NWR, SD |
| 295 | Jackson Lake NWR, ND |
| 306 | Lake George NWR, ND |
| 307 | Lake Ilo NWR, ND |
| 308 | Lake Nettie NWR, ND |
| 310 | Lake Zahl NWR, ND |
| 314 | McLean NWR, ND |
| 318 | Buffalo Lake NWR, ND |
| 320 | Hobart Lake NWR, ND |
| 322 | Susquehanna NWR, MD |
| 323 | Edwin B. Forsythe NWR, NJ |
| 324 | Stewart Lake NWR, ND |
| 325 | Lake Alice NWR, ND |
| 328 | Maxalee NWR, MS |
| 330 | Little White Salmon NFH, WA |
| 334 | Enfott NWR, WA |
| 335 | Winthrop NFH, WA |
| 340 | Havasu NWR, AZ & CA |
| 341 | San Andres NWR, NM |
| 342 | Horicon NWR, WI |
| 349 | Tualatin NWR, ND |
| 350 | Willow Lake NWR, ND |
| 350-1 | Imperial NWR, AZ & CA |
| 352 | Lake Merion NWR, KY & TN |
| 356 | Reelfoot NWR, KY & TN |
| 359 | Crescenta NWR, ND |
| 361 | Crossoprairie NWR, FL |
| 363 | Parker River NWR, MA |
| 364 | Santee NWR, SC |
| 365 | Moccasin River NWR, CA |
| 369 | Halfbreed Lake NWR, MT |
| 370 | Crosmeer NWR, MT |
| 392 | Mingo NWR, MO |
| 393 | Columbia NWR, WA |
| 394 | Slade NWR, ND |
| 395 | Creston NFH, MT |
| 396 | Sutter NWR, CA |
| 400 | J.N. "Ding" Darling NWR, FL |
| 401 | Tennessee NWR, TN |
| 403 | Fishermango NWR, OK |
| 404 | Hagerman NWR, TX |
| 406 | Laguna Atascosa NWR, TX |
| 412 | Michigan Islands NWR, MI |
| 413 | Matthew NWR, WA |
| 415 | Crab Orchard NWR, IL |
| 419 | Stillwater NWR, NV |
| 423 | North Attleboro NFH, MA |
| 424 | Spring Creek NWR, WA |
| 426 | Bo Cole NFH, CA |
| 428 | Nicerdine Forest NFH, MI |
| 429 | Penthitis Creek NFH, MI |
| 430 | Baldhill Dam NFH, ND |
| 433 | Preston NWR, FL |
| 434 | Amami NFH, WA |
| 435 | Arthur Marshall Loxahatchee NWR, FL |
| 438 | Monte Vista NWR, CO |
| 451 | Presquile NWR, VA |
| 452 | Eagle Creek NFH, OR |
| 458 | Shiawassee NWR, MI |
| 459 | National Key Deer Refuge, FL |
| 461 | Kirwin NWR, KS |
| 467 | Martin NWR, MD & VA |
| 468 | Elizabeth A. Morton NWR, NY |
| 477 | Quivira NWR, KS |
| 482 | Hickory NWR, AR |
| 483 | Norfolk NFH, AR |
| 487 | Audubon NWR, ND |
| 492 | Goose Point NFH, SD |
| 498 | Hale Bend NWR, IA & NE |
| 501 | Abernathy Fish Technology Cen., WA |
| 501-1 | Jackson NFH, WY |
| 505 | Irogicis NWR, NM |
| 505-2 | Klamath Forest NWR, OR |
| 507 | Cottselbourg NFH, VA |
| 513 | Dwlvey NWR, LA |
| 516 | War Horse NWR, MT |
| 517 | Buffalo Lake NWR, TX |
| 518 | DeSoto NWR, IA & NE |
| 519 | DeSoto NWR, IA & NE |
| 522 | Fish Springs NWR, UT |
| 523 | Erie NWR, PA |
| 529 | Willow Beach NFH, AZ |
| 531 | Mackay NWR, AZ |
| 538 | Kern NWR, CA |
| 541 | Great Swamp NWR, NJ |
| 542 | Modoc NWR, CA |
| 543 | Ouray NWR, UT |
| 547 | Jordan River NFH, MI |
| 549 | San Juan Islands NWR, WA |
| 550 | Mackay Islands NWR, NC & VA |
| 551 | Wapanocca NWR, AR |
| 555 | Washita NWR, OK |
| 566-1 | Garrison Dam NFH, ND |
| 566-1 | Garrison Dam NFH, ND |
| 571 | Detroit River NWR, MI |
| 581 | Wytheville NFH, VA |
| 589 | Harris Neck NWR, GA |
| 601 | Jones Hole NFH, UT |
| 603 | Deleron NWR, NV |
| 605 | Cross Creeks NWR, TN |
| 606 | Eastern Neck NWR, MD |
| 608 | Dale Hollow NFH, TN |
| 612 | Anahuac NWR, TX |
| 615 | John Heinz NWR at Tinicum, PA |
| 619 | Greens Ferry NFH, AR |
| 623 | Beulah Fish Technology Center, WY |
| 626 | Alamosa NWR, CO |
| 629 | Pjatunapant NWR, NV |
| 630 | Prime Hook NWR, DE |
| 632 | Merritt Island NWR, FL |
| 643 | Lake Woodruff NWR, FL |
| 651 | Choctaw NWR, AL |
| 655 | Lee Metcalf NWR, MT |
| 664 | Toppenish NWR, WA |
| 666 | Pee Dee NWR, NC |
| 674 | Clarence Cannon NWR, MO |
| 675 | Cedar Island NWR, NC |
| 676 | Cibola NWR, AZ & CA |
| 679 | Modeno NWR, CA |
| 680 | Eufaula NWR, AL & GA |
| 683 | Hatchie NWR, TN |
| 684 | Cedar Point NWR, OH |
| 687 | Conboy Lake NWR, WA |
| 690 | Lahonton NFH, NV |
| 690-1 | Quinault NFH, WA |
| 691 | Dworshak NFH, ID |
| 732 | Browns Park NWR, CO |
| 733 | Kooskia NFH, ID |
| 734 | Sherburne NWR, MN |
| 736 | Seedskadee NWR, WY |
| 745 | Hotchkiss NFH, CO |
| 746 | William L. Finley NWR, OR |
| 747 | Ankeny NWR, OR |
| 748 | Bassett Slough NWR, OR |
| 749 | Rachel Carson NWR, ME |
| 751 | San Luis NWR, CA |
| 752 | Warm Springs NFH, OR |
| 753 | Arapaho NWR, CO |
| 754 | Mattapeag Poss NWR, FL |
| 755 | Colorenhatchee NWR, FL |
| 761 | Maxwell NWR, NM |
| 763 | Flint Hills NWR, KS |
| 766 | Mascoutucks NWR, TN |
| 768 | Brazoria NWR, TX |
| 770 | Rachel Carson NWR, ME |
| 771 | San Luis NFH, CA |
| 772 | Malson Neck NWR, VA |
| 788 | Arapaho NWR, CO |
| 789 | UL Bend NWR, NY |
| 791 | Target Rock NWR, NY |
| 792 | St. Vincent NWR, FL |
| 794 | Green Lake NFH, ME |
| 795 | Bear Lake NWR, ID |
| 796 | Buck Island NWR, VI |
| 800 | Flatterman Island NWR, VA |
| 801 | Mason Neck NWR, VA |
| 803 | Mason Neck NWR, VA |
| 804 | San Bernard NWR, TX |
| 805 | Amagansett NWR, NY |
| 806 | Oyster Bay NWR, NY |
| 807 | Hobe Sound NWR, FL |
| 809 | Umatilla NWR, OR & WA |
| 810 | Seqluck NWR, OR |
| 811 | Massow NWR, GA |
| 814 | Grulla NWR, NM & TX |
| 825 | Sequoyah NWR, OK |
| 827 | Navigrt NWR, RI |

---

NFH — National Fish Hatchery
NWR — National Wildlife Refuge
WMA — Wildlife Management Area

# KEY TO REAL PROPERTY NUMBERS

## SEPTEMBER 30, 2008

NFH    National Fish Hatchery
NWR   National Wildlife Refuge
WMA  Wildlife Management Area

831 San Marcos NFH, TX
834 St. Johns NWR, FL
835 Conscience Point NWR, NY
836 Julia Butler Hansen NWR, OR & WA
838 Allegheny NFH, PA
839 Midway Valley NWR, RI
840 Southeast Point NWR, RI
842 Plum Tree Island NWR, VA
843 Saddle Mountain NWR, WA
845 Lewis and Clark NWR, OR
846 Nomans Land Island NWR, MA
847 Wapack NWR, NH
848 Seal Island NWR, ME
849 Thacher Island NWR, MA
850 Attwater Prairie Chicken NWR, TX
851 Menefacsia NWR, FL
852 Pond Island NWR, ME
853 Montezuma NWR, MA
855 Honolulu NWR, HI
856 Humboldt Bay NWR, CA
857 Swan River NWR, MT
858 Great Dismal Swamp NWR, NC & VA
859 Nisqually NWR, WA
860 Occoquan Bay NWR, VA
861 Wallops Island NWR, VA
862 White River NFH, VT
863 Rose Atoll NWR (Pacific Area Inset)
864 Franklin Island NWR, ME
865 Block Island NWR, RI
867 Amagansett Popfish Station, NY
868 Nomansend NWR, VA
870 San Pablo Bay NWR, CA
871 Nisqually Key NWR, FL
872 Sevilleta NWR, NM
876 Oxbow NWR, MA
877 Cabo Rojo NWR, PR
878 Baker Island NWR (Pacific Area Inset)
879 Howland Island NWR (Pacific Area Inset)
880 Jarvis Island NWR (Pacific Area Inset)
881 Petit Manan NWR, ME
882 Moïch NFH, WA
883 Supawna Meadows NWR, NJ
884 Egmont Key NWR, FL
889 Trustom Pond NWR, RI
890 Hopper Mountain NWR, CA
898 San Francisco Bay NWR, CA
900 Optima NWR, OK
901 Hillside NWR, MS
903 Big Stone NWR, MN
904 Moody NWR, TX
906 Seal Beach NWR, CA
907 Felsenthal NWR, AR
908 D'Arbonne NWR, LA
909 Mississippi Sandhill Crane NWR, MS
910 Karl E. Mundt NWR, NB & SD
911 Pearl Harbor NWR, HI
914 Pinckney Island NWR, SC
915 Ellicott Slough NWR, HI
920 Desecheo NWR, PR
921 James Campbell NWR, HI
923 Iron River NFH, WI
924 Salinas River NWR, CA
925 Morgan Brake NWR, MS
926 Panther Swamp NWR, MS
928 Green Cay NWR, VI
929 Bear Valley NWR, OR
930 Browns Wind Cane NWR, AL
931 Upper Ouachita NWR, LA
937 Featherstone NWR, VA

939 Fox River NWR, WI
940 Lower Suwannee NWR, FL
942 Crosswinds WMA, CA
943 Moapa Valley NWR, NV
944 Crocodile Lake NWR, FL
948 Bon Secour NWR, AL
949 McFaddin NWR, TX
950 Texas Point NWR, TX
965 Antioch Dunes NWR, CA
966 Butte Sink WMA, CA
967 Lower Hatchie NWR, TN
970 Kirtland Warbler NWR, MI
971 Cross Island NWR, ME
973 Mathews Brake NWR, MS
974 Bayou Lake NWR, GA
977 Overflow NWR, AR
981 Castle Rock NWR, CA
982 Tijuana Slough NWR, CA
984 Lower Rio Grande Valley NWR, TX
985 Watercress Darter NWR, AL
988 Bogue Chitto NWR, LA & MS
991 Alaska Maritime NWR, AK
992 Alaska Peninsula NWR, AK
993 Arctic NWR, AK
994 Becharof NWR, AK
995 Izembek NWR, AK
996 Kanuti NWR, AK
997 Kenai NWR, AK
998 Kodiak NWR, AK
999 Koyukuk NWR, AK
1000 Koyukuk NWR, AK
1001 Nowitna NWR, AK
1002 Selawik NWR, AK
1003 Tetlin NWR, AK
1004 Togiak NWR, AK
1005 Yukon Delta NWR, AK
1006 Yukon Flats NWR, AK
1008 Bears Bluff NFH, SC
1009 Fern Cave NWR, AL
1012 Richard Cronin NFH, MA
1015 San Bernardino NWR, AZ
1016 Ash Ridge NWR, CA
1018 Tensas River NWR, LA
1019 Protection Island NWR, WA
1021 Bandon Marsh NWR, OR
1024 Big Boggy NWR, TX
1025 Mandalay NWR, LA
1026 Crystal River NWR, FL
1027 Pierce—Celess Fish Facility, CA
1028 Siletz Bay NWR, OR
1029 Harbor Island NWR, MI
1030 Ash Meadows NWR, NV
1031 Alligator River NWR, NC
1032 Eastern Shore of Virginia NWR, VA
1034 San Simeon Field Station, CA
1035 Sonny Point NWR, VI
1036 Currituck NWR, NC
1037 Kilauea Point NWR, HI
1038 Buenos Aires NWR, AZ
1039 Stewart B. McKinney NWR, CT
1040 Chickasaw NWR, TN
1042 Bitter Creek NWR, CA
1043 Willow Creek—Lurline WMA, CA
1044 Coachella Valley NWR, CA
1046 Hanalei Forest NWR, OK
1051 Cache River NWR, AR
1052 Stringfellow NWR, FL
1053 Sleeper Lake NWR, WA
1054 AlcoñAlzayo NWR, LA
1056 Little River NWR, OK

1057 John Hay NWR, NH
1060 Little Sandy NWR, TX
1062 Pilot Knob NWR, MO
1063 San Joaquin River NWR, CA
1065 Midway Atoll NWR (Hawaii Inset)
1066 Lake Ophelia NWR, LA
1075 McFaddin NWR, TX
1076 San Diego Bay NWR, CA
1078 Sunnahage Meadows NWR, ME
1084 Cameron Prairie NWR, LA
1091 Logan Cave NWR, AR
1092 Florida Panther NWR, FL
1093 Cape May NWR, NJ
1094 Pettaquamscutt Cove NWR, RI
1113 Laguna Cartagena NWR, PR
1115 Sacramento River NWR, CA
1119 Bond Swamp NWR, GA
1122 St Catherine Creek NWR, MS
1124 Bayou Sauvage NWR, LA
1125 Pocosin Lakes NWR, NC
1126 Lyons Ferry NFH, WA
1127 Sawtooth NFH, ID
1129 Driftless Area NWR, IA
1132 Cypress Creek NWR, IL
1137 Grand Bay NWR, AL & MS
1138 Hamden Slough NWR, MN
1139 Roanoke River NWR, SC
1140 Ace Basin NWR, SC
1142 Franz Lake NWR, WA
1143 Greys Harbor NWR, WA
1149 Ohio River Islands NWR, KY, PA & WV
1153 James River NWR, VA
1154 Dahomey NWR, MS
1155 Tallahatchie NWR, MS
1156 Tucannon NFH, WA
1158 Nestucca Bay NWR, OR
1159 Neal Smith NWR, IA
1161 Archie Carr NWR, FL
1166 Grand Cote NWR, LA
1171 Ozark Cavefish NWR, MO
1174 Wallkill River NWR, NJ & NY
1175 North Central Valley WMA, CA
1176 Rydell NWR, MN
1178 Balcones Canyonlands NWR, TX
1179 Bayou Cocodrie NWR, LA
1180 Marin Islands NWR, CA
1181 Monterosa Lake NWR, NY
1182 Grand Cote NWR, LA
1183 Mora NFH, NM
1184 Siletz Bay NWR, OR
1185 Ten Ponds NWR, CO
1186 Morales Des Cygnes NWR, KS
1187 Great Bay NWR, NH
1189 Lake Umbagog NWR, ME & NH
1190 Tualatin River NWR, OR
1193 Handy Brake NWR, LA
1196 Kealia Pond NWR, HI
1199 Bill Williams NWR, AZ
1200 Leslie Canyon NWR, AZ
1207 Crane Meadows NWR, MN
1208 Guam NWR (Pacific Area Inset)
1209 Bald Knob NWR, AR
1210 Deep Fork NWR, IL
1213 Emiquon NWR, IL
1216 Coldwater Meadows NWR, WY
1218 Trinity River NWR, TX
1224 Loxer Woods Ridge NWR, FL
1225 Canada Valley NWR, WV
1226 Pipes Creek NWR, LA

1229 Rocky Mountain Arsenal NWR, CO
1231 Big Branch Marsh NWR, LA
1232 Stone Lakes NWR, CA
1235 Big Muddy Nat. Fish & Wildlife Refuge, MO
1241 Wallkoree NWR, MA
1244 Rappahannock R. NWR, VA
1245 San Diego NWR, CA
1247 Mandalay NWR, LA
1250 Ouray NFH, UT
1258 Ten Thousand Islands NWR, FL
1259 Key Cave NWR, AL
1261 Black Bayou Lake NWR, LA
1262 Bogue Chute NWR, NE
1267 Silvio O. Conte Nat. Fish & Wild. Ref., MA, NH & VT
1268 Waccamaw NWR, SC
1269 Maggie Valley Hatchery, ID
1270 Eagle (Fish) Lab, ID
1271 Blackfoot Valley WMA, MT
1272 Clarks River NWR, KY
1274 Deerlodge NFH, ID
1275 Livingston Stone NFH, CA
1276 Oregon Fish Hatchery & Satellites, OR
1277 Leavenworth Fish Hatchery, WA
1278 Aroostook NWR, ME
1279 Colorado River WMA, UT
1280 Lost Trail NWR, MT
1281 Nowitna Island NWR, BQ
1282 Shiawquorla Grasslands NWR, NY
1283 Whittlesey Creek NWR, WI
1284 Port Louisa NWR, IA & IL
1285 Great River NWR, IL & MO
1286 Two Rivers NWR, IL & MO
1287 Middle Mississippi River NWR, IL & MO
1289 Big Oak NWR, IA
1290 Cat Island NWR, LA
1291 John W. & Louise Seier NWR, NE
1292 Goodtague–Nipomo Dunes NWR, CA
1293 North Dakota WMA, ND
1294 Clearwater NWR, ID
1295 Northern Tallgrass Prairie NWR, MN
1296 Colchester River NWR, MS
1297 Oahu Forest NWR, HI
1298 Cahto Forest NWR, TX
1299 Palmyra Atoll NWR (Pacific Area Inset)
1300 Kingman Reef NWR (Pacific Area Inset)
1301 Assabet NWR, MA
1302 Vieques NWR, PR
1303 Dakota Tallgrass Prairie, ND & SD
1309 Bayou Teche NWR, LA
1311 Red River NWR, LA
1312 Cahaba River NWR, AL
1313 Boca NWR, CO
1314 Mountain Longleaf NWR, AL
1315 Theodore Roosevelt NWR, MS
1316 Holt Collier NWR, MS
1317 Glacial Ridge NWR, MN
1319 Neches River NWR, TX
1320 Rocky Mountain Front, MT

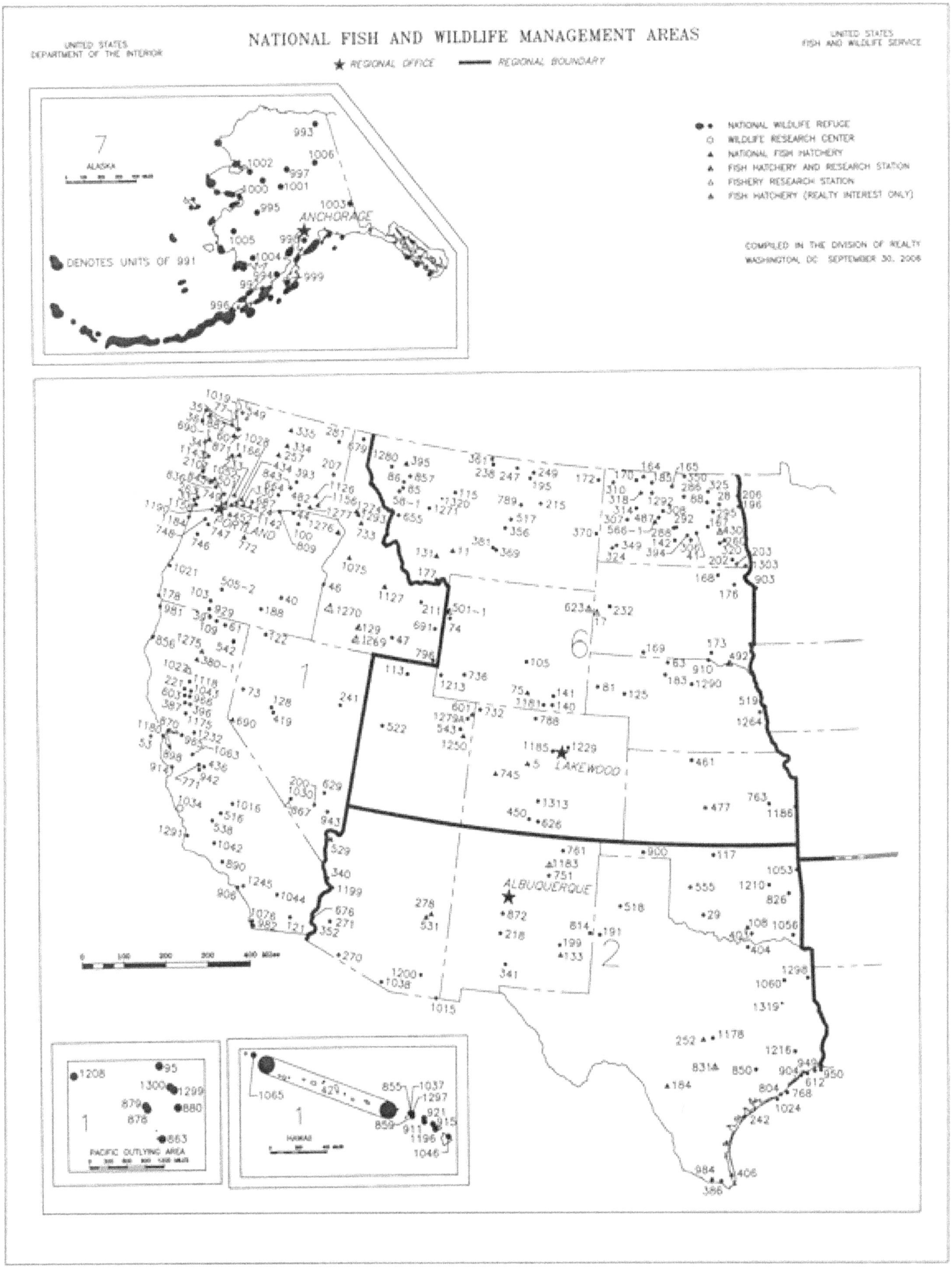

UNITED STATES
DEPARTMENT OF THE INTERIOR
NATIONAL FISH AND WILDLIFE MANAGEMENT AREAS
REGIONAL OFFICE
REGIONAL BOUNDARY
UNITED STATES
FISH AND WILDLIFE SERVICE
NATIONAL WILDLIFE REFUGE
WILDLIFE RESEARCH CENTER
NATIONAL FISH HATCHERY
FISH HATCHERY AND RESEARCH STATION
FISHERY RESEARCH STATION
FISH HATCHERY (REALTY INTEREST ONLY)
COMPILED IN THE DIVISION OF REALTY
WASHINGTON, DC SEPTEMBER 30, 2006
ALASKA
ANCHORAGE
DENOTES UNITS OF 991
PORTLAND
LAKEWOOD
ALBUQUERQUE
PACIFIC OUTLYING AREA
HAWAII

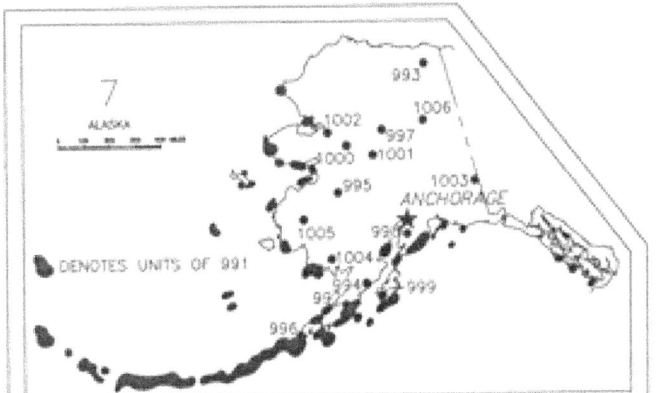

# NATIONAL FISH AND WILDLIFE MANAGEMENT AREAS

REGIONAL OFFICE ——— REGIONAL BOUNDARY

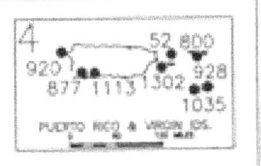

PUERTO RICO & VIRGIN IDS.

NAVASSA ISLAND

● ● NATIONAL WILDLIFE REFUGE
○ WILDLIFE RESEARCH CENTER
▲ NATIONAL FISH HATCHERY
▲ FISH HATCHERY AND RESEARCH STATION
△ FISHERY RESEARCH STATION
▲ FISH HATCHERY (REALTY INTEREST ONLY)

COMPILED IN THE DIVISION OF REALTY
WASHINGTON, DC   SEPTEMBER 30, 2006

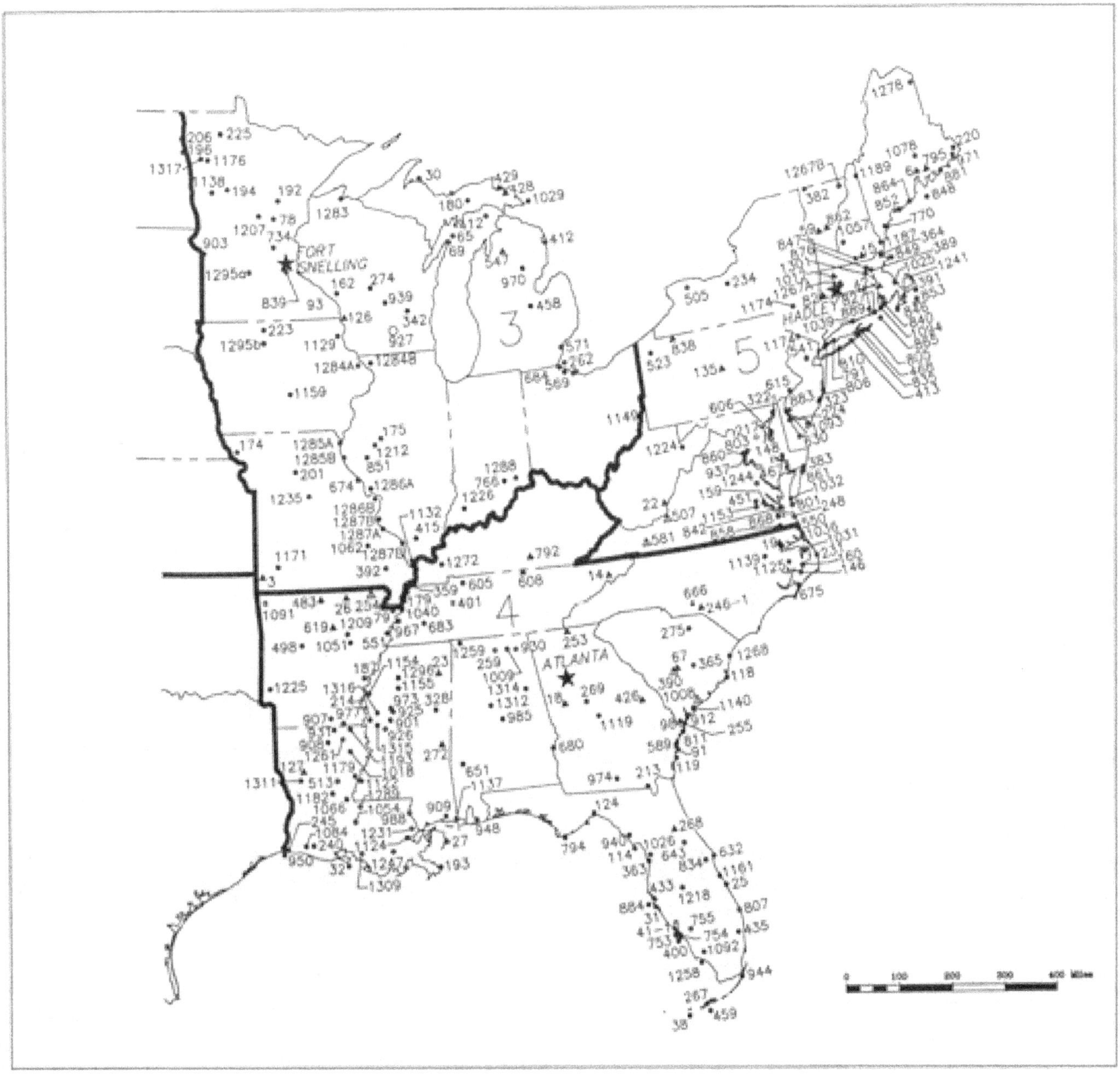

## U.S. Fish & Wildlife Service

### Wetland Management Districts of the National Wildlife Refuge System
Idaho, Iowa, Maine, Michigan, Minnesota, Montana, Nebraska, North Dakota, South Dakota, Wisconsin

*Waterfowl Production Area Counties*

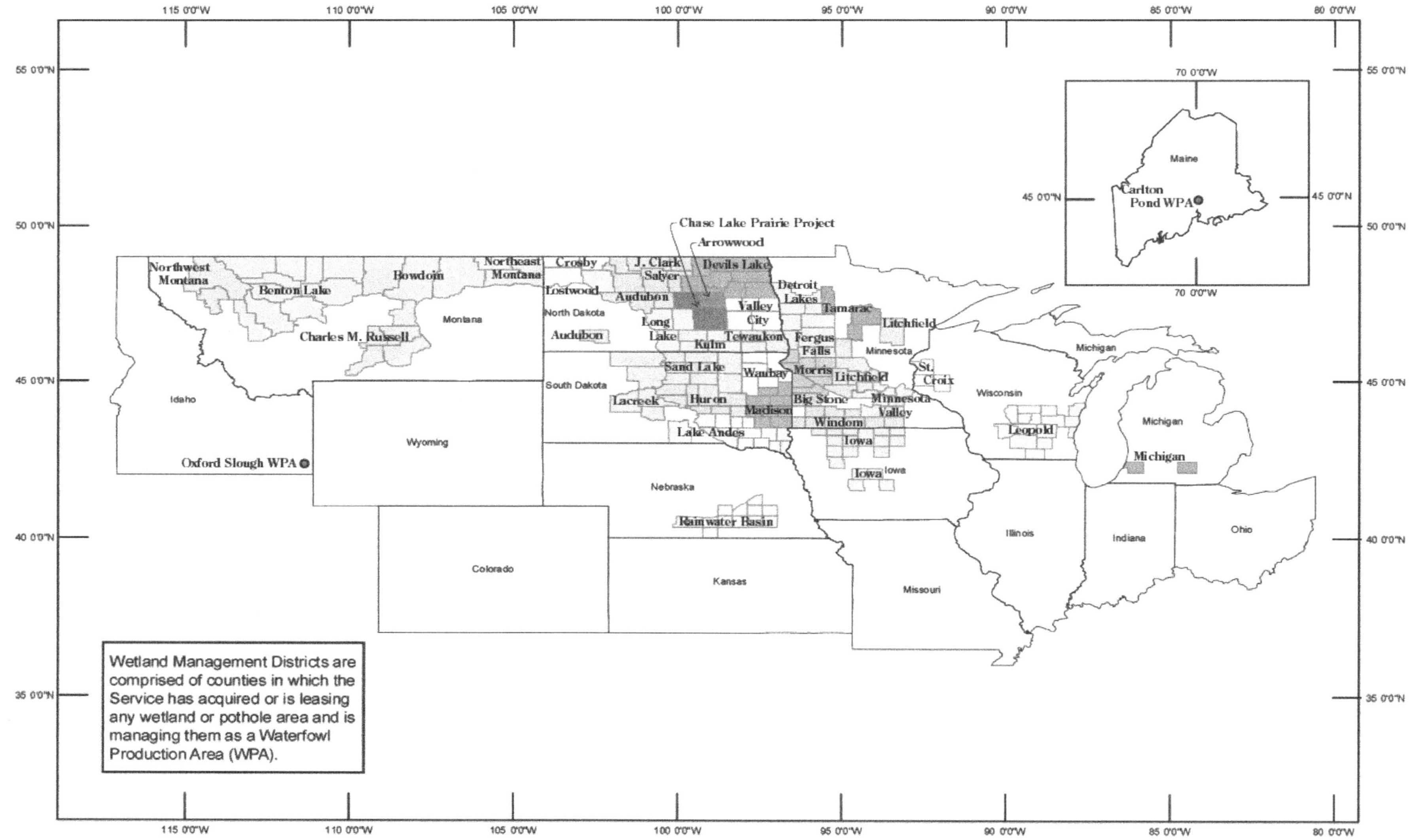

WGS 1984

Wetland Management Districts are comprised of counties in which the Service has acquired or is leasing any wetland or pothole area and is managing them as a Waterfowl Production Area (WPA).

PRODUCED IN THE DIVISION OF REALTY
WASHINGTON, D.C.
LAND STATUS CURRENT TO: 9/30/2006
BASEMAP: ESRI
DATUM: WGS 1984
MAP NAME: WMDs2006

# Significant Land Acquisition Accomplishments in Fiscal Year 2006

The U.S. Fish and Wildlife Service acquired fee title or other interest in more than 116,000 acres of land in Fiscal Year 2006. The Service also added two new units to the National Wildlife Refuge System, **Neches River National Wildlife Refuge** in Texas and **Rocky Mountain Front Conservation Area** in Montana, increasing the total number of national wildlife refuges from 545 to 547.

## Pacific Region

On June 15, 2006, President George W. Bush issued Presidential Proclamation 8031 establishing the **Northwestern Hawaiian Islands Marine National Monument,** a 1,200-mile stretch of spectacular coral islands, seamounts, banks, and shoals. The 140,000-acre Monument encompasses both the **Hawaiian Islands National Wildlife Refuge** and the **Midway Atoll National Wildlife Refuge,** both of which provide permanent protection and conservation of habitat for the endangered Hawaiian monk seal, the threatened Hawaiian green sea turtle, and other rare marine species. The area is also home to millions of nesting seabirds. The Fish and Wildlife Service co-manages the Monument with the National Oceanic and Atmospheric Administration, and has sole responsibility for management of the refuges.

## Southwest Region

A 3,082.04 acre tract at the **San Bernard National Wildlife Refuge** in Texas was the largest addition to the National Wildlife Refuge System in FY 2006. The Service purchased 2,832.66 acres, and acquired 249.74 acres by donation, an accomplishment that resulted from the close cooperation and partnership with the National Fish and Wildlife Foundation. The refuge is a productive and valuable wetland complex that provides wintering, migration, and resident habitat for waterfowl, wading birds, neo-tropical migratory birds, and other wetland-dependent species, in a rapidly developing area south of Houston.

## Great Lakes-Big Rivers Region

At the **Northern Tallgrass Prairie National Wildlife Refuge,** the Service acquired 1,241.07 acres of habitat easements and 16.13 acres of fee ownership, bringing the total number of acres owned to 4,071.59. The Legislative Committee for Minnesota Resources helped to facilitate the acquisition of several key fee and easement tracts. Partners such as the Brandenburg Prairie Foundation and The Nature Conservancy also assisted the Service in its acquisition and protection efforts. The Service acquires land in 85 counties in western Minnesota and northwestern Iowa for the refuge, and plans to acquire approximately 77,000 additional fee and easement acres from willing sellers. In addition, the Service is working with private landowners to develop stewardship agreements and is also providing incentives and management assistance for preservation of the prairie landscape to all interested owners. The prairie preservation and restoration project not only protects the prairie ecosystem but also benefits grassland birds as well.

The American Land Conservancy (ALC) contributed 658.97 acres of key habitat for a wide range of migratory bird species, as part of the Rockwood Island Donation, to the Middle Mississippi River National Wildlife Refuge. ALC also constructed and donated a headquarters building for the refuge. The lands at this refuge are unique, having been acquired in response to the great flood of 1993 and lying within the uncontrolled portion of the Middle Mississippi River below the confluence with the Missouri River. River levels in this "open river" section of the Mississippi are not regulated by the lock and dam system, and water levels may fluctuate greatly; there is frequent flooding on the refuge.

The **Sauk County Waterfowl Production Area** was established with a single purchase of 210.88 acres. Located in south-central Wisconsin, the Waterfowl Production Area is part of a larger cooperative conservation project called

Fairfield Marsh Conservation Project. The Service partnered with a community-based group of local, State, and Federal agencies, special interest groups, and landowners that call themselves FACT (Farming and Conservation Together), to provide conservation and restoration alternatives to landowners within the project area.

## Southeast Region

We added 6,723 acres of seasonally-flooded bottomland in one of the most important and vulnerable wetland areas of the Mississippi River Delta were to the **Catahoula National Wildlife Refuge** in east central Louisiana through the efforts of a partnership comprised of Wal-Mart's "Acres for America" program, The Conservation Fund, American Electric Power, the National Fish and Wildlife Foundation, and the Service. The adjacent Catahoula Lake is one of only 22 wetland sites in the United States recognized by the Ramsar Convention as a Wetland of International Importance. This acquisition will help secure the future of the refuge and support the on-going objective of providing habitat for native and migratory waterfowl and other wildlife, including the more than 175 wetland-dependent bird species.

In southeastern Georgia, the Service accepted The Conservation Fund's donation of approximately 6,782 acres that we added to the **Okefenokee National Wildlife Refuge**. The property had been part of a 16,000-acre tract purchased in 1994 by the DuPont Corporation and was initially proposed to be strip-mined for titanium oxide deposits. Following years of negotiations with local officials and interest groups, a "no-mining" option was selected; DuPont agreed to retire without compensation the mineral rights associated with the tract. DuPont, through its Land Legacy Program, then donated the property to The Conservation Fund (TCF), and TCF, in turn, donated 6,782 acres to the Service for the refuge. The upland pine habitat on the property will support threatened and endangered species such as the red-cockaded woodpecker and the eastern indigo snake.

Working with the Trust for Public Land, the Service acquired another 1,875 acres in a multi-year land acquisition/carbon sequestration project at **Tensas River National Wildlife Refuge** in Louisiana. Prior to this acquisition, the refuge consisted of two noncontiguous forested units totaling approximately 65,000 acres separated by agricultural land. Completion of this project and restoration of the native bottomland hardwood forest will reconnect the refuge units, thereby increasing the size and contiguity of forested refuge lands that provide habitat for a variety of species including the threatened Louisiana black bear. In addition to TPL, partners on this project have included Entergy Services, Inc., The Detroit Edison Company, and The Nature Conservancy.

This year the Service acquired 615 acres from the Louisiana Department of Wildlife and Fisheries (LDWF), for the **Black Bayou Lake National Wildlife Refuge** in Louisiana. Prior to this acquisition, the Service managed the property as part of the Refuge under a lease with LDWF. Established in 1997 through a unique partnership with the city of Monroe, the Refuge consists of pristine wetlands associated with a 2,000-acre shallow, cypress-studded lake, riparian areas, and reforested cropland. The lake and adjacent wetlands are vital wintering habitat for migratory waterfowl, primarily mallard, pintail, redhead, canvasback, and scaup. The extensive stands of buttonbush, cypress, and tupelo trees provide ideal breeding and brood-rearing habitat for resident wood duck. Acquisition of the LDWF property almost completes the Service's acquisition at this refuge, with only three private ownerships remaining within the refuge boundary.

### Northeast Region
The Service acquired the last remaining privately owned inholding within the boundary of the **Petit Manan National Wildlife Refuge**'s Gouldsboro Bay Division in Maine, completing the 621-acre Division. The property includes two potential building lots and a road right-of-way through the refuge. The Division habitat consists of spruce-fir forests, shrub and herbaceous upland, and intertidal wetlands. The coast supports nesting bald eagles. Black ducks, great blue herons, and American bitterns utilize the saltmarsh; semipalmated sandpipers, dowitchers, greater and lesser yellowlegs, and dunlins probe the mudflats for invertebrates.

The Service and the Trust for Public Land partnered in the acquisition of 23 acres in the Fort River Division of **Silvio O. Conte National Fish and Wildlife Refuge**. This was the first acquisition in the Fort River Division; it contains significant river frontage along the longest free-flowing tributary of the Connecticut River in Massachusetts. Working with TPL has enabled the Service to complement and expand the mosaic of conserved grassland and riparian habitat in the Fort River area. The combined efforts of the partners will benefit plants, fish, wildlife, and people by conserving critical habitat, protecting water quality in the vicinity of a municipal well, and creating outdoor recreational opportunities within a rapidly developing area.

The Service acquired 30 acres of the 82-acre Dixon tract at **Eastern Shore of Virginia National Wildlife Refuge**. Close cooperation among the Service, The Nature Conservancy's Virginia Coastal Reserve, and the Virginia Department of Conservation and Recreation facilitated completion of this acquisition. These partners also assisted the Service with protecting the nearby 496-acre TNC/Bull Tract. The Service acquired the first 210 acres of that tract with funds from the Land and Water Conservation Fund, Migratory Bird Conservation Fund, and the North American Wetlands Conservation Act funds.

### Mountain-Prairie Region
The Service established the **Rocky Mountain Front Conservation Area** in north-central Montana by purchasing a 4,177-acre conservation easement in partnership with The Nature Conservancy, and the landowner donated part of the tract's value.

The Service accepted a transfer of 7,258 acres from the Department of the Army for the **Rocky Mountain Arsenal National Wildlife Refuge** in Colorado. Like the 4,930 acres previously transferred to the Service, these 7,258 acres were decontaminated before transfer. Upon completion of decontamination of an additional 3,985 acres, the Department of the Army will transfer those acres also to the Service. The refuge is one of the largest urban wildlife refuges in the United States; it consists of open lakes, wetlands, prairie grasslands, and woodlands. The refuge supports over 330 species of mammals, birds, reptiles, amphibians, and fish.

### Alaska Region
The Service purchased a 79.96-acre parcel on the banks of Cane Creek, for the **Arctic National Wildlife Refuge** in Alaska. The parcel provides habitat for grizzly bears, moose, caribou, wolves, and furbearers such as beaver, marten, wolverines, and river otters. Dall sheep inhabit the surrounding mountains, and the mountains are also important wintering areas for the Porcupine herd of caribou.

The Service purchased a 159.99-acre parcel in the **Innoko National Wildlife Refuge** in Alaska. Located on the east bank of Hather Creek and the west bank of Magitchlie Creek, about three miles upstream from the Innoko River, the parcel provides prime winter habitat for moose and black bears, as well as breeding habitat for waterfowl. The area also provides important furbearer habitat throughout the year. In addition, the sloughs and backwaters surrounding this parcel are important northern pike and whitefish summer habitat.

The Service acquired four tracts totaling 519.92 acres, for addition to the **Togiak National Wildlife Refuge** in Alaska. These tracts include high-quality stream habitat that supports all five species of Alaska salmon. In addition, the area provides habitat for brown bear, moose, and caribou, as well as nesting and breeding habitat for numerous species of migratory waterfowl. This acquisition includes 199.97 acres located in the Togiak Wilderness.

The Service acquired six tracts totaling 1,079.73 acres for the **Yukon Flats National Wildlife Refuge** in Alaska. The tracts contain several habitat types, including high-quality wetlands that support nesting and breeding for migratory waterfowl and excellent habitat for moose—an important subsistence resource for local residents. These areas also benefit neo-tropical migratory songbirds.

TABLE 1 - SUMMARY BY CATEGORIES

| CATEGORY | | RESERVED FROM PUBLIC DOMAIN | | ACQUIRED BY OTHER FEDERAL AGENCY | | DEVISE OR GIFT | PURCHASED | | AGREEMENT EASEMENT OR LEASE | TOTAL ACRES |
|---|---|---|---|---|---|---|---|---|---|---|
| | | SOLE OR PRIMARY | SECONDARY | SOLE OR PRIMARY | SECONDARY | | ACRES | COST ($) | | |
| NATIONAL WILDLIFE REFUGES | 547 | 81,325,231.35 | 635,400.29 | 3,160,468.38 | 1,210,809.23 | 751,913.75 | 4,272,396.06 | 1,920,173,475.17 | 1,452,495.23 | 92,808,715.26 |
| WATERFOWL PRODUCTION AREAS | 204 | 15,897.64 | 0.00 | 26,758.41 | 0.00 | 15,899.85 | 695,476.77 | 213,340,208.99 | 2,491,397.15 | 3,245,429.82 |
| COORDINATION AREAS | 50 | 56,586.61 | 0.00 | 139,273.47 | 55,739.14 | 0.00 | 681.13 | 13,480.00 | 63,544.00 | 315,824.35 |
| TOTAL | 801 | 81,397,715.60 | 635,400.29 | 3,326,501.24 | 1,266,548.37 | 767,813.60 | 4,968,553.96 | 2,133,527,164.16 | 4,007,436.35 | 96,369,969.43 |
| ADMINISTRATIVE SITES | 46 | 50.31 | 36.00 | 9.40 | 2.39 | 0.75 | 1,038.72 | 11,334,769.05 | 41.88 | 1,179.45 |
| NATIONAL FISH HATCHERIES | 69 | 3,607.09 | 987.09 | 2,467.68 | 3,707.30 | 1,358.94 | 5,404.06 | 3,518,401.59 | 4,341.42 | 21,873.58 |
| TOTAL | 115 | 3,657.40 | 1,023.09 | 2,477.08 | 3,709.69 | 1,359.69 | 6,442.78 | 14,853,170.64 | 4,383.30 | 23,053.03 |
| GRAND TOTAL | 916 | 81,401,373.00 | 636,423.38 | 3,328,978.32 | 1,270,258.06 | 769,173.29 | 4,974,996.76 | 2,148,380,334.80 | 4,011,819.65 | 96,360,022.46 |

REPORT DEFINITIONS

THE FOLLOWING DEFINITIONS ARE USED SOLELY FOR ADMINISTRATIVE PURPOSES IN GROUPING LAND USE CATEGORIES FOR THIS REPORT AND DO NOT NECESSARILY REFLECT THE DEFINITIONS FOUND IN 50 CFR 25.12

ADMINISTRATIVE SITE: LAND USED TO SUPPORT ADMINISTRATIVE PROGRAMS, SUCH AS MAINTENANCE FACILITIES OR OFFICES, AND OFF-SITE VISITOR CENTERS (TABLE 6).

COORDINATION AREA: ANY AREA ADMINISTERED AS PART OF THE NATIONAL WILDLIFE REFUGE SYSTEM AND MANAGED BY THE STATE UNDER COOPERATIVE AGREEMENTS BETWEEN THE SERVICE AND A STATE FISH AND WILDLIFE AGENCY (TABLE 5).

MIGRATORY WATERFOWL REFUGE ON A FEDERAL WATER RESOURCE PROJECT: FEDERAL LAND MANAGED BY THE SERVICE AS PART OF THE NATIONAL WILDLIFE REFUGE SYSTEM TO MITIGATE A FEDERAL WATER RESOURCE PROJECT FOR THE BENEFIT OF MIGRATING WATERFOWL (AND OTHER WILDLIFE) UNDER THE FISH AND WILDLIFE COORDINATION ACT (TABLE 9).

NATIONAL FISH HATCHERY: FACILITY WHERE FISH ARE RAISED. HATCHERY OBJECTIVES ARE TO REPLENISH DEPLETED STOCKS, TO MITIGATE FEDERAL WATER PROJECTS, TO ASSIST WITH THE MANAGEMENT OF FISHERY RESOURCES ON FEDERAL (PRIMARILY SERVICE) AND INDIAN LANDS, AND TO ENHANCE RECREATIONAL FISHERIES (TABLE 7).

NATIONAL WILDLIFE REFUGE: ANY AREA OF THE NATIONAL WILDLIFE REFUGE SYSTEM, EXCEPT COORDINATION AREAS AND WATERFOWL PRODUCTION AREAS (TABLE 3).

WATERFOWL PRODUCTION AREA: ANY WETLAND OR POTHOLE AREA ACQUIRED PURSUANT TO THE MIGRATORY BIRD HUNTING AND CONSERVATION STAMP ACT OR OTHER STATUTORY AUTHORITY AND ADMINISTERED AS PART OF THE NATIONAL WILDLIFE REFUGE SYSTEM AND IDENTIFIED BY COUNTY DESIGNATION (TABLE 4).

WILDERNESS AREA: SERVICE LAND DESIGNATED BY CONGRESS TO BE MANAGED AS A UNIT OF THE NATIONAL WILDERNESS PRESERVATION SYSTEM, IN ACCORDANCE WITH THE TERMS OF THE WILDERNESS ACT OF 1964. ALL SERVICE WILDERNESS AREAS OCCUR WITHIN NATIONAL WILDLIFE REFUGES, WITH THE EXCEPTION OF MOUNT MASSIVE WILDERNESS AREA WHICH IS LOCATED AT THE LEADVILLE NATIONAL FISH HATCHERY (TABLE 8).

NOTE: FOR CONVERSION TO METRIC UNITS
1 ACRE = .405 HECTARES

TABLE 2 - SUMMARY BY STATES, ASSOCIATED GOVERNMENTS AND POSSESSIONS

| STATE | | RESERVED FROM PUBLIC DOMAIN | | ACQUIRED BY OTHER FEDERAL AGENCY | | DEVISE OR GIFT | PURCHASED | | AGREEMENT EASEMENT OR LEASE | TOTAL ACRES |
|---|---|---|---|---|---|---|---|---|---|---|
| | | SOLE OR PRIMARY | SECONDARY | SOLE OR PRIMARY | SECONDARY | | ACRES | COST ($) | | |
| ALABAMA | 11 | 0.00 | 0.00 | 16,114.00 | 37,521.62 | 2,471.89 | 13,318.34 | 30,260,225.00 | 1,462.89 | 71,188.24 |
| ALASKA | 47 | 76,311,595.11 | 13,369.10 | 3.00 | 2.36 | 58,014.71 | 386,678.35 | 136,058,011.65 | 202,309.14 | 76,819,563.41 |
| ARIZONA | 16 | 1,548,669.60 | 27,270.45 | 4,212.93 | 12,501.23 | 1,200.00 | 124,311.01 | 18,301,215.00 | 9,367.20 | 1,727,532.42 |
| ARKANSAS | 13 | 8,851.60 | 0.00 | 103,976.82 | 823.73 | 2,999.22 | 581,206.20 | 15,742,204.99 | 1,125.02 | 309,100.17 |
| CALIFORNIA | 42 | 81,573.38 | 45,118.29 | 36,496.77 | 6,467.84 | 51,585.60 | 156,616.11 | 214,417,262.56 | 134,157.17 | 472,515.16 |
| COLORADO | 12 | 97,780.57 | 0.00 | 16,523.70 | 2,054.99 | 933.33 | 102,075.89 | 26,471,754.36 | 24,279.90 | 168,268.31 |
| CONNECTICUT | 2 | 0.00 | 0.00 | 0.00 | 4.90 | 263.56 | 692.71 | 23,022,590.00 | 1.72 | 962.89 |
| DELAWARE | 2 | 0.00 | 0.00 | 141.80 | 0.00 | 62.11 | 24,466.67 | 9,117,774.88 | 903.19 | 26,173.47 |
| FLORIDA | 30 | 4,863.76 | 154.00 | 32,467.54 | 138,262.70 | 4,438.96 | 235,527.77 | 131,032,504.45 | 562,321.51 | 978,025.54 |
| GEORGIA | 12 | 0.00 | 0.00 | 76,311.96 | 3,276.90 | 33,967.62 | 408,341.44 | 3,042,011.04 | 3,097.52 | 489,172.09 |
| HAWAII | 13 | 254,418.10 | 0.00 | 72.80 | 61.15 | 91.38 | 44,013.73 | 40,086,004.60 | 834.32 | 299,491.48 |
| IDAHO | 15 | 32,193.17 | 23,943.40 | 2,096.42 | 205.14 | 181.06 | 21,347.61 | 4,057,302.86 | 16,619.76 | 192,097.43 |
| ILLINOIS | 11 | 66.15 | 0.00 | 46,187.61 | 67,556.28 | 4,818.11 | 32,468.77 | 18,093,685.73 | 444.81 | 151,530.73 |
| INDIANA | 5 | 0.00 | 0.00 | 215.03 | 51,000.00 | 412.55 | 13,413.51 | 8,924,892.50 | 0.00 | 65,045.42 |
| IOWA | 27 | 333.68 | 0.00 | 0.00 | 47,237.94 | 81.22 | 67,933.80 | 48,158,229.71 | 712.01 | 116,298.63 |
| KANSAS | 5 | 0.00 | 0.00 | 176.10 | 29,241.21 | 262.20 | 29,170.29 | 5,620,934.30 | 4.37 | 58,756.48 |
| KENTUCKY | 3 | 0.00 | 0.00 | 0.00 | 20.47 | 0.00 | 10,369.00 | 8,414,899.15 | 0.00 | 10,379.47 |
| LOUISIANA | 24 | 10,882.62 | 2,892.83 | 248,701.50 | 0.00 | 29,803.53 | 291,591.06 | 129,272,883.16 | 10,029.94 | 571,978.12 |
| MAINE | 12 | 0.00 | 0.00 | 12,077.59 | 0.00 | 4,347.51 | 48,740.48 | 40,482,428.72 | 767.13 | 65,932.71 |
| MARYLAND | 11 | 0.00 | 0.00 | 11,690.89 | 0.00 | 3,949.39 | 26,961.25 | 18,360,963.23 | 98.21 | 45,725.94 |
| MASSACHUSETTS | 12 | 0.00 | 0.00 | 4,464.53 | 0.00 | 720.69 | 16,653.46 | 22,796,648.74 | 71.58 | 25,900.26 |
| MICHIGAN | 13 | 2,990.54 | 521.70 | 7,678.64 | 1,080.52 | 574.02 | 102,149.54 | 11,319,041.00 | 1,864.95 | 179,267.68 |
| MINNESOTA | 60 | 268.18 | 0.00 | 165,924.76 | 15,674.87 | 6,274.33 | 297,843.28 | 111,881,749.06 | 81,412.37 | 567,417.89 |
| MISSISSIPPI | 14 | 4.00 | 0.00 | 80,527.97 | 3,070.45 | 5,116.04 | 132,180.41 | 76,163,175.00 | 70,461.90 | 225,428.79 |
| MISSOURI | 12 | 0.00 | 0.00 | 11,067.98 | 13,607.00 | 121.97 | 48,587.76 | 12,636,731.12 | 258.43 | 73,563.74 |
| MONTANA | 34 | 437,134.96 | 380,852.77 | 365,947.62 | 114,525.01 | 6,785.67 | 90,314.16 | 32,124,626.68 | 212,134.19 | 1,386,142.91 |
| NEBRASKA | 17 | 15,796.88 | 2,684.81 | 70,215.85 | 0.00 | 5,880.82 | 81,420.24 | 16,016,760.74 | 3,525.51 | 179,314.11 |
| NEVADA | 11 | 2,242,938.96 | 18,201.20 | 4.45 | 523.20 | 4,779.11 | 94,125.92 | 25,445,246.25 | 10,392.22 | 2,416,266.08 |
| NEW HAMPSHIRE | 5 | 0.00 | 0.00 | 1,054.00 | 0.00 | 1,806.60 | 18,418.39 | 14,626,218.99 | 251.21 | 21,510.20 |
| NEW JERSEY | 4 | 0.00 | 0.00 | 6.89 | 5.56 | 4,511.60 | 66,680.35 | 117,733,371.60 | 3,061.75 | 73,270.33 |
| NEW MEXICO | 10 | 15,766.26 | 57,215.48 | 0.00 | 438.52 | 220,200.00 | 90,697.96 | 5,317,667.69 | 733.67 | 385,051.89 |
| NEW YORK | 12 | 0.00 | 0.00 | 1,829.19 | 0.00 | 6,824.04 | 19,087.39 | 11,286,119.67 | 1,548.61 | 29,189.23 |
| NORTH CAROLINA | 12 | 0.00 | 0.00 | 50,964.86 | 11.38 | 237,790.66 | 129,553.13 | 38,413,609.52 | 9,989.41 | 428,309.43 |
| NORTH DAKOTA | 133 | 16,581.60 | 0.00 | 172,436.43 | 14,952.69 | 5,496.00 | 320,266.20 | 29,848,420.36 | 1,211,198.54 | 1,706,741.56 |
| OHIO | 3 | 77.53 | 0.00 | 0.00 | 0.00 | 2,445.42 | 5,960.39 | 4,433,893.56 | 598.20 | 9,081.14 |
| OKLAHOMA | 12 | 77,960.20 | 0.00 | 522.80 | 61,294.08 | 142.30 | 29,250.54 | 13,776,794.77 | 3,061.89 | 170,897.56 |
| OREGON | 28 | 267,561.70 | 4,608.28 | 63,079.93 | 9,826.80 | 6,409.47 | 225,872.56 | 47,469,470.70 | 849.14 | 578,206.88 |
| PENNSYLVANIA | 2 | 0.00 | 0.00 | 32.26 | 45.04 | 243.14 | 9,695.41 | 9,372,752.75 | 0.00 | 10,070.85 |
| RHODE ISLAND | 5 | 0.00 | 0.00 | 581.96 | 0.00 | 630.89 | 1,086.59 | 20,136,700.00 | 156.39 | 2,455.83 |
| SOUTH CAROLINA | 7 | 0.00 | 0.00 | 84,214.62 | 100.00 | 5,907.93 | 60,147.29 | 29,447,610.90 | 22,894.16 | 175,273.40 |
| SOUTH DAKOTA | 51 | 1,848.76 | 0.00 | 28,782.89 | 581.00 | 16,322.74 | 163,495.64 | 29,532,247.79 | 1,258,035.95 | 1,480,066.98 |
| TENNESSEE | 6 | 0.00 | 0.00 | 7,825.87 | 38,312.96 | 96.69 | 63,141.72 | 36,335,190.95 | 15,692.04 | 120,208.21 |

TABLE 2 - SUMMARY BY STATES, ASSOCIATED GOVERNMENTS AND POSSESSIONS

| STATE | | RESERVED FROM PUBLIC DOMAIN | | ACQUIRED BY OTHER FEDERAL AGENCY | | DEVISE OR GIFT | PURCHASED | | AGREEMENT EASEMENT OR LEASE | TOTAL ACRES |
|---|---|---|---|---|---|---|---|---|---|---|
| | | SOLE OR PRIMARY | SECONDARY | SOLE OR PRIMARY | SECONDARY | | ACRES | COST ($) | | |
| TEXAS | 23 | 0.00 | 0.00 | 46,944.97 | 13,521.80 | 14,699.61 | 451,817.91 | 209,039,188.76 | 54,076.47 | 581,070.56 |
| UTAH | 9 | 65,783.84 | 0.00 | 2,382.94 | 0.00 | 4,276.45 | 34,813.66 | 4,582,572.72 | 5,252.38 | 112,515.19 |
| VERMONT | 4 | 0.00 | 0.00 | 0.00 | 0.00 | 346.38 | 32,806.92 | 7,497,047.37 | 86.00 | 30,319.28 |
| VIRGINIA | 14 | 0.00 | 0.00 | 5,941.36 | 0.00 | 53,594.95 | 70,712.26 | 83,975,241.25 | 5,901.55 | 136,185.54 |
| WASHINGTON | 39 | 40,466.42 | 2,182.11 | 34,874.66 | 187,347.02 | 1,588.67 | 71,415.30 | 42,342,229.58 | 8,803.04 | 346,722.42 |
| WEST VIRGINIA | 4 | 0.00 | 0.00 | 18.90 | 0.00 | 313.97 | 18,665.95 | 45,283,960.10 | 29.04 | 19,427.84 |
| WISCONSIN | 27 | 747.93 | 0.00 | 96,468.37 | 40,341.00 | 200.64 | 97,839.74 | 26,337,019.43 | 38.40 | 236,636.08 |
| WYOMING | 16 | 23,207.56 | 11,501.57 | 16,079.93 | 13,548.63 | 4,518.67 | 26,676.36 | 11,747,701.76 | 7,104.47 | 102,838.13 |
| AMERICAN SAMOA | 1 | 0.00 | 37,453.00 | 1,613.00 | 0.00 | 0.00 | 0.00 | 0.00 | 0.00 | 39,066.00 |
| GUAM | 1 | 0.00 | 0.00 | 772.10 | 0.00 | 0.00 | 0.00 | 0.00 | 22,456.00 | 23,228.10 |
| U.S. MINOR OUTLYING ISLANDS | 8 | 0.00 | 0.00 | 1,695,367.81 | 282,835.00 | 0.00 | 443.95 | 9,500,000.00 | 2.30 | 1,978,649.06 |
| PUERTO RICO | 5 | 0.00 | 0.00 | 20,527.96 | 0.00 | 0.00 | 1,269.36 | 2,999,295.63 | 787.10 | 22,584.46 |
| VIRGIN ISLANDS | 3 | 0.00 | 0.00 | 46.07 | 0.00 | 0.00 | 544.08 | 3,784,370.00 | 0.00 | 590.15 |
| GRAND TOTAL | 917 | 81,401,373.00 | 636,423.38 | 3,326,978.32 | 1,270,258.06 | 769,173.29 | 4,974,996.76 | 2,148,380,330.80 | 4,011,819.65 | 96,393,022.46 |

| STATE | | RESERVED FROM PUBLIC DOMAIN | | ACQUIRED BY OTHER FEDERAL AGENCY | | DEVISE OR GIFT | PURCHASED | | AGREEMENT EASEMENT OR LEASE | TOTAL ACRES |
|---|---|---|---|---|---|---|---|---|---|---|
| | | SOLE OR PRIMARY | SECONDARY | SOLE OR PRIMARY | SECONDARY | | ACRES | COST ($) | | |
| ALASKA | 11 | 0.00 | 0.00 | 2.00 | 2.39 | 0.00 | 2,088.40 | 1,250,000.00 | 0.39 | 2,093.18 |
| ARIZONA | 2 | 0.00 | 0.00 | 0.00 | 0.00 | 0.00 | 0.41 | 20,000.00 | 1,921.40 | 1,921.81 |
| ARKANSAS | 2 | 0.00 | 0.00 | 0.00 | 0.00 | 0.00 | 1,295.10 | 1,980,000.00 | 0.00 | 1,295.10 |
| CALIFORNIA | 5 | 0.00 | 0.00 | 198.00 | 0.00 | 58.91 | 385.82 | 4,640,000.00 | 3,716.10 | 4,298.83 |
| COLORADO | 3 | 1,178.57 | 0.00 | 7,258.00 | -7,258.00 | 0.00 | 0.00 | 0.00 | 90.00 | 1,268.57 |
| CONNECTICUT | 2 | 0.00 | 0.00 | 0.00 | 0.00 | 16.10 | 30.75 | 369,000.00 | 0.00 | 46.85 |
| FLORIDA | 2 | 0.00 | 0.00 | 0.00 | 0.00 | 0.00 | 2.29 | 711,802.00 | 0.00 | 2.29 |
| GEORGIA | 1 | 0.00 | 0.00 | 0.00 | 0.00 | 6,781.91 | 0.00 | 0.00 | 0.00 | 6,781.91 |
| IDAHO | 1 | 0.00 | 0.00 | 0.00 | 0.00 | 0.00 | 0.00 | 1.00 | 0.00 | 0.00 |
| ILLINOIS | 2 | 0.00 | 0.00 | 0.00 | 0.00 | 658.97 | 9.06 | 58,000.00 | 0.00 | 668.03 |
| INDIANA | 1 | 0.00 | 0.00 | 0.00 | 0.00 | 0.00 | 183.07 | 212,700.00 | 0.00 | 183.07 |
| IOWA | 10 | 0.00 | 0.00 | 0.00 | 0.00 | 0.00 | 1,163.63 | 4,029,606.00 | 0.00 | 1,163.63 |
| KENTUCKY | 1 | 0.00 | 0.00 | 0.00 | 0.00 | 0.00 | 380.83 | 564,300.00 | 0.00 | 380.83 |
| LOUISIANA | 6 | 0.00 | 0.00 | 0.00 | 0.00 | 6,272.84 | 2,600.14 | 2,800,400.00 | -6,881.54 | 2,041.44 |
| MAINE | 3 | 0.00 | 0.00 | 0.00 | 0.00 | 0.00 | 6.41 | 960,600.00 | 52.19 | 58.60 |
| MASSACHUSETTS | 2 | 0.00 | 0.00 | 0.00 | 0.00 | 0.00 | 33.10 | 1,676,900.00 | 0.00 | 33.10 |
| MICHIGAN | 2 | 0.00 | 0.00 | 0.00 | 0.00 | 138.41 | 0.00 | 0.00 | 2,244.50 | 2,382.91 |
| MINNESOTA | 22 | 0.00 | 0.00 | 0.00 | 0.00 | 56.58 | 1,360.76 | 3,205,678.00 | 3,039.27 | 4,456.62 |
| MISSISSIPPI | 5 | 0.00 | 0.00 | -2,018.98 | 0.00 | 0.00 | 691.50 | 3,675.00 | 0.00 | -1,325.48 |
| MISSOURI | 2 | 0.00 | 0.00 | 0.00 | 0.00 | 0.00 | 501.95 | 810,500.00 | 0.00 | 501.95 |
| MONTANA | 8 | 0.00 | 0.00 | 0.00 | 0.00 | 0.00 | 680.00 | 272,000.00 | 15,339.45 | 16,019.45 |
| NEBRASKA | 1 | 0.00 | 0.00 | 0.00 | 0.00 | 0.04 | 0.00 | 0.00 | 0.00 | 0.04 |
| NEVADA | 3 | 0.00 | 0.00 | 0.00 | 0.00 | 0.00 | 241.43 | 1,549,000.00 | 0.00 | 241.43 |
| NEW HAMPSHIRE | 2 | 0.00 | 0.00 | 0.00 | 0.00 | 0.00 | 51.01 | 254,000.01 | 0.00 | 51.01 |
| NEW JERSEY | 5 | 0.00 | 0.00 | 0.00 | 0.00 | 250.65 | 169.59 | 1,609,000.00 | 0.00 | 420.24 |
| NORTH DAKOTA | 26 | 0.00 | 0.00 | 0.00 | 0.00 | 0.00 | 344.67 | 168,001.00 | 34,232.72 | 34,577.39 |
| OKLAHOMA | 1 | 0.00 | 0.00 | 0.00 | 0.00 | 0.00 | 70.03 | 22,500.00 | 0.00 | 70.03 |
| OREGON | 2 | 0.00 | 0.00 | 0.00 | 0.00 | 0.00 | 93.96 | 490,540.00 | 0.00 | 93.96 |
| RHODE ISLAND | 1 | 0.00 | 0.00 | 0.00 | 0.00 | 0.00 | 7.26 | 560,000.00 | 0.19 | 7.45 |
| SOUTH CAROLINA | 1 | 0.00 | 0.00 | 0.00 | 0.00 | 0.00 | 859.68 | 2,109,096.70 | 0.00 | 859.68 |
| SOUTH DAKOTA | 23 | 0.00 | 0.00 | 0.00 | 0.00 | 0.00 | 22.50 | 22,500.00 | 28,549.70 | 28,572.20 |
| TENNESSEE | 1 | 0.00 | 0.00 | 0.00 | 0.00 | 87.73 | 448.50 | 768,400.00 | 0.00 | 536.23 |
| TEXAS | 8 | 0.00 | 0.00 | 288.10 | -288.10 | 0.00 | 5,482.50 | 5,780,482.74 | 253.06 | 5,735.56 |
| UTAH | 1 | 0.00 | 0.00 | 0.00 | 0.00 | 0.00 | 33.43 | 308,044.00 | 0.00 | 33.43 |
| VERMONT | 2 | 0.00 | 0.00 | 0.00 | 0.00 | 0.00 | 50.10 | 107,000.00 | 0.00 | 50.10 |
| VIRGINIA | 2 | 0.00 | 0.00 | 0.00 | 0.00 | 0.00 | 70.31 | 2,700,000.00 | 0.00 | 70.31 |
| WASHINGTON | 4 | 0.00 | 0.00 | 0.00 | 0.00 | 337.00 | 141.96 | 347,501.00 | 0.00 | 478.96 |
| WEST VIRGINIA | 1 | 0.00 | 0.00 | 0.00 | 0.00 | 0.00 | 16.88 | 190,000.00 | 0.00 | 16.88 |
| WISCONSIN | 7 | 0.00 | 0.00 | 0.00 | 0.00 | 26.00 | 455.58 | 1,584,000.00 | 0.00 | 481.58 |
| U.S. MINOR OUTLYING ISLANDS | 1 | 0.00 | 0.00 | 0.00 | 0.00 | 0.00 | 28.20 | 600,000.00 | 0.00 | 28.20 |
| GRAND TOTAL | 190 | 1,178.57 | 0.00 | 5,845.12 | -7,541.71 | 14,845.15 | 19,582.95 | 42,839,027.45 | 82,515.43 | 115,995.51 |

TABLE 3 - NATIONAL WILDLIFE REFUGES

| STATE AND UNIT | RESERVED FROM PUBLIC DOMAIN | | ACQUIRED BY OTHER FEDERAL AGENCY | | DEVISE OR GIFT | PURCHASED | | AGREEMENT EASEMENT OR LEASE | TOTAL ACRES |
|---|---|---|---|---|---|---|---|---|---|
| | SOLE OR PRIMARY | SECONDARY | SOLE OR PRIMARY | SECONDARY | | ACRES | COST ($) | | |
| **ALABAMA** | | | | | | | | | |
| BON SECOUR | 0.00 | 0.00 | 32.34 | 0.00 | 135.05 | 6,260.93 | 22,723,644.00 | 720.00 | 7,148.32 |
| CAHABA RIVER | 0.00 | 0.00 | 0.00 | 0.00 | 0.00 | 3,414.09 | 5,680,416.00 | 0.00 | 3,414.09 |
| CHOCTAW | 0.00 | 0.00 | 0.00 E | 4,218.00 | 0.00 | 0.00 | 0.00 | 0.00 | 4,218.00 |
| EUFAULA | (1) | 0.00 | 0.00 | 0.00 E | 7,929.00 | 0.00 | 24.19 | 80,000.00 | 0.00 | 7,953.19 |
| FERN CAVE | 0.00 | 0.00 | 0.00 | 0.00 | 0.00 | 199.23 | 110,000.00 | 0.00 | 199.23 |
| FSA INTEREST AL | 0.00 | 0.00 | 0.00 | 0.00 | 0.00 | 0.00 | 0.00 | 742.69 | 742.69 |
| GRAND BAY | (27) | 0.00 | 0.00 | 0.00 | 0.00 | 895.86 | 1,822.00 | 710,613.00 | 0.00 | 2,717.86 |
| KEY CAVE | 0.00 | 0.00 | 0.00 | 0.00 | 0.00 | 1,060.00 | 0.00 | 0.00 | 1,060.00 |
| MOUNTAIN LONGLEAF | 0.00 | 0.00 | 7,758.68 | 0.00 | 1,257.00 | 0.00 | 0.00 | 0.00 | 9,015.68 |
| SAUTA CAVE | 0.00 | 0.00 | 0.00 | 0.00 | 0.00 | 264.00 | 575,000.00 | 0.00 | 264.00 |
| WATERCRESS DARTER | 0.00 | 0.00 | 0.00 | 0.00 | 0.00 | 24.52 | 230,850.00 | 0.00 | 24.52 |
| WHEELER | 0.00 | 0.00 | 8,322.98 T | 25,674.62 | 183.68 | 249.39 | 149,700.00 | 0.00 | 34,430.66 |
| STATE TOTAL | 15 | 0.00 | 0.00 | 96,114.00 | 37,821.62 | 2,471.59 | 13,318.34 | 30,260,225.00 | 1,462.69 | 71,186.24 |
| **ALASKA** | | | | | | | | | |
| ALASKA MARITIME | 3,370,632.44 N | 9,099.00 | 0.00 | 0.00 | 0.00 | 11,035.02 | 7,677,891.80 | 26,990.45 | 3,417,756.91 |
| ALASKA PENINSULA | 3,496,905.00 | 0.00 | 0.00 | 0.00 | 50,948.87 | 56,634.92 | 2,000,106.00 | 0.34 | 3,560,489.13 |
| ARCTIC | 19,260,110.00 | 0.00 | 0.00 | 0.00 | 0.00 | 23,211.94 | 198,000.00 | 0.40 | 19,286,322.34 |
| BECHAROF | 1,200,000.00 | 0.00 | 0.00 | 0.00 | 0.00 | 80.27 | 267,300.00 | 0.00 | 1,200,060.27 |
| INNOKO | 3,850,000.00 | 0.00 | 0.00 | 0.00 | 0.00 | 479.98 | 292,500.00 | 1.07 | 3,850,481.05 |
| IZEMBEK | 302,201.00 N | 860.00 | 0.00 | 0.00 | 7,961.78 | 0.00 | 0.00 | 0.00 | 311,075.78 |
| KANUTI | 1,430,000.00 | 0.00 | 0.00 | 0.00 | 0.00 | 159.91 | 68,000.00 | 0.26 | 1,430,160.17 |
| KENAI | 1,904,472.00 | 0.00 | 0.00 | 0.00 | 0.00 | 7,923.07 | 10,619,299.96 | 30.33 | 1,912,425.40 |
| KODIAK | 1,656,169.40 | 0.00 | 0.00 | 0.00 | 883.33 | 175,357.53 | 105,912,995.84 | 157,860.66 | 1,990,270.92 |
| KOYUKUK | 3,560,000.00 | 0.00 | 0.00 | 0.00 | 0.00 | 159.96 | 98,000.00 | 0.31 | 3,560,160.27 |
| NOWITNA | 1,560,000.00 | 0.00 | 0.00 | 0.00 | 0.00 | 0.00 | 0.00 | 0.00 | 1,560,000.00 |
| SELAWIK | 2,150,000.00 | 0.00 | 0.00 | 0.00 | 0.00 | 159.98 | 56,000.00 | 2.01 | 2,150,161.99 |
| TETLIN | 700,000.00 | 0.00 | 0.00 | 0.00 | 0.00 | 5.00 | 15,500.00 | 53.54 | 700,058.54 |
| TOGIAK | 4,097,430.00 | 0.00 | 0.00 | 0.00 | 0.00 | 3,746.34 | 4,536,000.00 | 1.29 | 4,101,177.63 |
| YUKON DELTA | 19,120,628.00 BIA | 63.00 | 0.00 | 0.00 | 0.00 | 24,238.00 | 0.00 | 17,357.90 | 19,162,296.90 |
| YUKON FLATS | 8,600,000.00 | 0.00 | 0.00 | 0.00 | 0.00 | 3,384.04 | 1,560,500.00 | 0.53 | 8,603,384.57 |
| STATE TOTAL | 16 | 76,241,567.84 | 10,085.00 | 0.00 | 0.00 | 59,853.98 | 305,565.96 | 133,300,087.60 | 202,298.69 | 76,919,281.47 |
| **ARIZONA** | | | | | | | | | |
| BILL WILLIAMS RIVER | 2,781.00 R | 943.07 | 0.00 R | 756.00 | 0.00 | 1,574.69 | 1,600,000.00 | 0.00 | 6,054.76 |
| BUENOS AIRES | 0.00 | 0.00 | 0.00 | 0.00 | 0.00 | 116,805.50 | 14,549,591.00 | 301.66 | 117,107.16 |
| CABEZA PRIETA | 860,000.00 | 0.00 | 0.00 | 0.00 | 0.00 | 41.32 | 18,300.00 | 0.00 | 860,041.32 |
| CIBOLA | (2) | 3,577.92 | 0.00 | 4,212.93 R | 623.38 | 0.00 | 191.81 | 362,000.00 | 0.00 | 8,606.04 |
| HAVASU | (2) | 19,004.54 R | 10,418.30 | 0.00 R | 9,816.98 | 0.00 | 40.00 | 8,000.00 | 0.00 | 39,279.82 |
| IMPERIAL | (2) | 0.00 R | 15,801.27 | 0.00 R | 1,304.87 | 0.00 | 643.62 | 201,724.00 | 0.00 | 17,809.76 |
| KOFA | 665,400.00 | 0.00 | 0.00 | 0.00 | 0.00 | 1,080.00 | 396,000.00 | 0.00 | 666,480.00 |
| LESLIE CANYON | 0.00 | 0.00 | 0.00 | 0.00 | 1,200.00 | 1,564.76 | 256,000.00 | 8,952.12 | 11,716.88 |
| SAN BERNARDINO | 0.00 | 0.00 | 0.00 | 0.00 | 0.00 | 2,367.87 | 830,600.00 | 0.70 | 2,368.57 |
| STATE TOTAL | 9 | 1,541,763.46 | 27,222.64 | 4,212.93 | 12,501.23 | 1,200.00 | 124,309.57 | 18,275,915.00 | 9,254.48 | 1,720,494.31 |
| **ARKANSAS** | | | | | | | | | |
| BALD KNOB | 0.00 | 0.00 | 0.00 | 0.00 | 0.00 | 14,809.95 | 9,250,000.00 | 0.00 | 14,809.95 |
| BIG LAKE | 8,875.60 | 0.00 | 1,597.34 | 0.00 | 0.00 | 562.91 | 31,854.69 | 0.25 | 11,036.10 |
| CACHE RIVER | 0.00 | 0.00 | 6,091.19 | 0.00 | 945.14 | 56,813.24 | 48,639,791.42 | 0.00 | 63,849.57 |
| FELSENTHAL | 0.00 | 0.00 | 64,813.34 | 0.00 | 0.00 | 88.80 | 100,000.00 | 0.00 | 64,902.14 |
| FSA INTEREST AR | 0.00 | 0.00 | 3,161.47 | 0.00 | 0.00 | 0.00 | 0.00 | 297.20 | 3,458.67 |
| HOLLA BEND | 0.00 | 0.00 | 4,068.00 | 0.00 | 28.85 | 2,201.45 | 339,983.00 | 0.73 | 6,299.03 |

13

TABLE 3 - NATIONAL WILDLIFE REFUGES

| STATE AND UNIT | | RESERVED FROM PUBLIC DOMAIN | | ACQUIRED BY OTHER FEDERAL AGENCY | | DEVISE OR GIFT | PURCHASED | | AGREEMENT EASEMENT OR LEASE | TOTAL ACRES |
|---|---|---|---|---|---|---|---|---|---|---|
| | | SOLE OR PRIMARY | SECONDARY | SOLE OR PRIMARY | SECONDARY | | ACRES | COST ($) | | |
| **ARKANSAS** | | | | | | | | | | |
| LOGAN CAVE | | 0.00 | 0.00 | 0.00 | 0.00 | 0.00 | 123.59 | 138,136.00 | 0.00 | 123.59 |
| OVERFLOW | | 0.00 | 0.00 | 0.00 | 0.00 | 0.00 | 13,042.89 | 10,607,020.50 | 0.00 | 13,042.89 |
| POND CREEK | | 0.00 | 0.00 | 0.00 E | 730.00 | 1,932.11 | 24,382.70 | 0.00 | 413.52 | 27,229.43 |
| WAPANOCCA | | 0.00 | 0.00 | 0.00 | 0.00 | 0.00 | 5,484.17 | 1,351,456.00 | 0.00 | 5,484.17 |
| WHITE RIVER | | 0.00 | 0.00 | 84,243.02 E | 45.80 | 1,093.12 | 72,949.68 | 5,464,190.37 | 413.22 | 158,749.82 |
| STATE TOTAL | 10 | 8,881.60 | 0.00 | 163,374.36 | 745.80 | 3,996.22 | 190,259.38 | 75,080,374.98 | 1,125.02 | 368,985.36 |
| **CALIFORNIA** | | | | | | | | | | |
| ANTIOCH DUNES | | 0.00 | 0.00 | 0.00 | 0.00 | 0.00 | 55.38 | 2,135,000.00 | 0.00 | 55.38 |
| BITTER CREEK | | 0.00 | 0.00 | 0.00 | 0.00 | 40.00 | 14,056.70 | 4,779,500.00 | 0.00 | 14,096.70 |
| BLUE RIDGE | | 0.00 | 0.00 | 0.00 | 0.00 | 0.00 | 897.08 | 642,500.00 | 0.00 | 897.08 |
| BUTTE SINK | | 0.00 | 0.00 | 0.00 | 0.00 | 0.00 | 732.86 | 3,850,700.00 | 10,310.64 | 11,043.50 |
| CASTLE ROCK | | 0.00 | 0.00 | 0.00 | 0.00 | 0.00 | 13.89 | 41,250.00 | 0.00 | 13.89 |
| CIBOLA | (3) | 1,258.00 | | 2,094.52 | 0.00 | 600.00 | 0.00 | 0.00 | 297.00 | 4,249.52 |
| CLEAR LAKE | | 0.00 R | 11,503.43 | 13,020.07 | 0.00 | 0.00 | 0.00 | 0.00 | 0.00 | 24,123.50 |
| COACHELLA VALLEY | | 0.00 | 0.00 | 0.00 | 0.00 | 1,029.51 | 2,548.10 | 9,313,908.77 | 0.00 | 3,577.61 |
| COLUSA | | 0.00 | 0.00 | 0.00 | 0.00 | 0.27 | 4,039.71 | 291,280.85 | 0.00 | 4,039.98 |
| DELEVAN | | 0.00 | 0.00 | 0.00 | 0.00 | 0.00 | 5,796.54 | 2,345,739.00 | 0.00 | 5,796.54 |
| DON EDWARDS SAN FRAN BAY | | 0.00 | 0.00 | 37.26 | 0.00 | 449.34 | 24,807.46 | 42,976,134.00 | 4,678.83 | 29,972.89 |
| ELLICOTT SLOUGH | | 0.00 | 0.00 | 0.00 | 0.00 | 0.00 | 164.44 | 971,000.00 | 28.11 | 198.55 |
| FARALLON | | 91.00 CG | 120.00 | 0.00 | 0.00 | 0.00 | 0.00 | 0.00 | 0.00 | 211.00 |
| FSA INTEREST CA | | 0.00 | 0.00 | 198.00 | 0.00 | 0.00 | 0.00 | 0.00 | 2.71 | 205.71 |
| GRASSLANDS | | 0.00 | 0.00 | 0.00 | 0.00 | 0.00 | 14,970.25 | 18,068,228.00 | 73,718.47 | 88,688.72 |
| GUADALUPE-NIPOMO DUNES | | 0.00 | 0.00 | 0.00 | 0.00 | 2,553.00 | 0.00 | 0.00 | 0.00 | 2,553.00 |
| HAVASU | (3) | 10.00 R | 4,160.23 | 0.00 R | 3,065.15 | 0.00 | 0.00 | 0.00 | 0.00 | 7,235.34 |
| HOPPER MOUNTAIN | | 0.00 | 0.00 | 0.00 | 0.00 | 0.00 | 2,471.00 | 640,000.00 | 0.00 | 2,471.00 |
| HUMBOLDT BAY | | 0.00 CG | 1.00 | 0.00 | 0.00 | 654.97 | 2,719.44 | 5,399,610.00 | 0.00 | 3,375.41 |
| IMPERIAL | (3) | 0.00 R | 6,309.05 | 0.00 R | 1,649.14 | 0.00 | 0.00 | 0.00 | 0.00 | 7,958.19 |
| KERN | | 0.00 | 0.00 | 0.00 | 0.00 | 631.00 | 10,618.17 | 579,912.00 | 0.00 | 11,249.17 |
| LOWER KLAMATH | (4) | 39,315.72 | 0.00 | 0.00 | 0.00 | 447.89 | 4,530.53 | 3,390,123.00 | 0.41 | 44,294.55 |
| MARIN ISLANDS | | 0.00 | 0.00 | 0.00 | 0.00 | 102.59 | 28.70 | 1,010,000.00 | 0.00 | 131.29 |
| MERCED | | 0.00 | 0.00 | 0.00 | 0.00 | 0.00 | 3,803.82 | 2,180,000.00 | 1.76 | 3,805.58 |
| MODOC | | 40.00 | 0.00 | 0.00 | 0.00 | 310.00 | 6,670.62 | 5,548,854.19 | 0.61 | 7,021.23 |
| NORTH CENTRAL VALLEY | | 0.00 | 0.00 | 0.00 | 0.00 | 0.00 | 2,398.46 | 4,052,752.00 | 13,309.11 | 15,687.57 |
| PIXLEY | | 0.00 | 0.00 | 4,521.05 | 0.00 | 170.00 | 2,274.56 | 2,203,713.00 | 4.55 | 6,970.16 |
| SACRAMENTO | | 0.00 | 0.00 | 0.00 | 0.00 | 35.66 | 10,783.34 | 162,968.00 | 0.00 | 10,819.00 |
| SACRAMENTO RIVER | | 0.00 | 0.00 | 0.00 | 0.00 | 258.39 | 9,231.42 | 28,623,370.66 | 1,286.41 | 10,816.22 |
| SALINAS RIVER | | 0.00 | 0.00 | 363.61 | 0.00 | 0.00 | 0.00 | 0.00 | 3.82 | 367.43 |
| SAN DIEGO | | 0.00 | 0.00 | 88.00 | 0.00 | 3,477.07 | 4,776.55 | 29,398,320.00 | 1.01 | 8,342.63 |
| SAN DIEGO BAY | | 0.00 | 0.00 | 0.00 | 0.00 | 414.80 | 0.00 | 0.00 | 2,200.00 | 2,614.80 |
| SAN JOAQUIN RIVER | | 0.00 | 0.00 | 0.00 | 0.00 | 0.00 | 7,147.65 | 25,725,448.00 | 2,946.97 | 10,094.62 |
| SAN LUIS | | 0.00 | 0.00 | 14,760.00 | 0.00 | 0.00 | 7,422.41 | 2,171,055.00 | 703.00 | 22,893.41 |
| SAN PABLO BAY | | 0.00 | 0.00 | 0.00 | 0.00 | 248.72 | 5,741.00 | 6,742,600.00 | 51,200.00 | 13,589.72 |
| SEAL BEACH | | 0.00 | 0.00 | 0.00 N | 852.17 | 0.00 | 0.00 | 0.00 | 58.54 | 910.71 |
| SONNY BONO SALTON SEA | | 0.00 R | 23,424.58 | 360.98 | 0.00 | 0.00 | 9,342.14 | 294,461.80 | 4,531.17 | 37,658.87 |
| STONE LAKES | | 0.00 | 0.00 | 0.00 | 0.00 | 121.14 | 1,625.76 | 6,236,621.50 | 3,101.34 | 4,848.24 |
| SUTTER | | 0.00 | 0.00 | 0.00 | 0.00 | 0.00 | 2,590.96 | 291,281.80 | 0.00 | 2,590.96 |
| TIJUANA SLOUGH | | 0.00 | 0.00 | 0.00 N | 981.42 | 1.25 | 406.08 | 7,888,000.00 | 65.00 | 1,023.75 |
| TULE LAKE | | 39,103.37 | 0.00 | 0.00 | 0.00 | 0.00 | 9.37 | 0.00 | 3.84 | 39,116.58 |
| WILLOW CREEK-LURLINE | | 0.00 | 0.00 | 0.00 | 0.00 | 0.00 | 0.00 | 0.00 | 5,586.50 | 5,586.50 |

TABLE 3 - NATIONAL WILDLIFE REFUGES

| STATE AND UNIT | | RESERVED FROM PUBLIC DOMAIN | | ACQUIRED BY OTHER FEDERAL AGENCY | | DEVISE OR GIFT | PURCHASED | | AGREEMENT EASEMENT OR LEASE | TOTAL ACRES |
|---|---|---|---|---|---|---|---|---|---|---|
| | | SOLE OR PRIMARY | SECONDARY | SOLE OR PRIMARY | SECONDARY | | ACRES | COST ($) | | |
| **CALIFORNIA** | | | | | | | | | | |
| STATE TOTAL | 38 | 79,823.09 | 45,118.29 | 36,441.49 | 6,117.84 | 11,585.60 | 198,593.59 | 214,264,041.56 | 134,093.80 | 470,773.70 |
| **COLORADO** | | | | | | | | | | |
| ALAMOSA | | 86.29 | 0.00 | 816.40 | 0.00 | 218.90 | 10,904.78 | 2,377,463.16 | 0.00 | 12,026.37 |
| ARAPAHO | | 4,782.54 | 0.00 | 0.00 | 0.00 | 0.00 | 18,461.33 | 4,930,296.00 | 27.53 | 23,271.40 |
| BACA | | 1,178.57 | 0.00 | 3,301.84 | 0.00 | 0.00 | 53,642.00 | 14,280,000.00 | 21,454.24 | 79,576.65 |
| BROWNS PARK | | 6,794.30 | 0.00 | 0.00 | 0.00 | 0.00 | 5,335.53 | 642,976.00 | 1,326.47 | 13,456.30 |
| COLORADO RIVER | (45) | 0.00 | 0.00 | 17.64 | 0.00 | 0.00 | 0.00 | 0.00 | 321.38 | 339.02 |
| FSA INTEREST CO | | 0.00 | 0.00 | 0.00 | 0.00 | 0.00 | 42.64 | 0.00 | 1,164.00 | 1,206.64 |
| MONTE VISTA | | 800.00 | 0.00 | 0.00 | 0.00 | 83.33 | 13,950.66 | 2,241,750.00 | 0.00 | 14,833.99 |
| ROCKY MOUNTAIN ARSENAL | | 0.00 | 0.00 | 12,187.85 A | 3,894.99 | 0.00 | 0.00 | 0.00 | 0.00 | 96,082.84 |
| TWO PONDS | | 0.00 | 0.00 | 0.00 | 0.00 | 7.10 | 64.94 | 3,948,103.20 | 0.00 | 72.04 |
| STATE TOTAL | 7 | 13,661.70 | 0.00 | 16,323.73 | 3,894.99 | 309.33 | 102,411.88 | 28,426,578.36 | 24,272.62 | 180,864.25 |
| **CONNECTICUT** | | | | | | | | | | |
| SILVIO O. CONTE | | 0.00 | 0.00 | 0.00 | 0.00 | 0.00 | 30.75 | 369,000.00 | 0.00 | 30.75 |
| STEWART B. MCKINNEY | | 0.00 | 0.00 | 0.00 CG | 4.90 | 263.56 | 661.96 | 22,653,590.00 | 1.72 | 932.14 |
| STATE TOTAL | 1 | 0.00 | 0.00 | 0.00 | 4.90 | 263.56 | 692.71 | 23,022,590.00 | 1.72 | 962.89 |
| **DELAWARE** | | | | | | | | | | |
| BOMBAY HOOK | | 0.00 | 0.00 | 541.50 | 0.00 | 0.00 | 15,436.26 | 1,637,738.90 | 80.00 | 16,057.76 |
| FSA INTEREST DE | | 0.00 | 0.00 | 0.00 | 0.00 | 0.00 | 0.00 | 0.00 | 2.60 | 2.60 |
| PRIME HOOK | | 0.00 | 0.00 | 0.00 | 0.00 | 32.11 | 9,210.41 | 7,480,035.78 | 870.59 | 10,113.11 |
| STATE TOTAL | 2 | 0.00 | 0.00 | 541.50 | 0.00 | 32.11 | 24,646.67 | 9,117,774.68 | 953.19 | 26,173.47 |
| **FLORIDA** | | | | | | | | | | |
| ARCHIE CARR | | 0.00 | 0.00 | 1.42 | 0.00 | 127.21 | 43.93 | 12,478,130.00 | 79.34 | 251.90 |
| ARTHUR R. MARSHALL | | 0.00 | 0.00 | 0.00 | 0.00 | 0.00 | 2,649.77 | 118,511.97 | 141,404.00 | 143,953.77 |
| CALOOSAHATCHEE | | 40.00 | 0.00 | 0.00 | 0.00 | 0.00 | 0.00 | 0.00 | 0.00 | 40.00 |
| CEDAR KEYS | | 378.61 | 0.00 | 0.00 | 0.00 | 0.00 | 342.54 | 681,180.00 | 170.00 | 891.15 |
| CHASSAHOWITZKA | | 320.56 | 0.00 | 0.00 | 0.00 | 0.00 | 30,522.35 | 496,746.12 | 0.00 | 30,842.91 |
| CROCODILE LAKE | | 0.00 | 0.00 | 4.20 | 0.00 | 40.63 | 6,521.65 | 13,092,544.00 | 125.76 | 6,692.24 |
| CRYSTAL RIVER | | 0.00 | 0.00 | 0.00 | 0.00 | 0.00 | 80.13 | 1,732,180.00 | 0.00 | 80.13 |
| EGMONT KEY | | 328.30 | 0.00 | 0.00 | 0.00 | 0.00 | 0.00 | 0.00 | 0.00 | 328.30 |
| FLORIDA PANTHER | | 0.00 | 0.00 | 0.00 | 0.00 | 594.00 | 25,935.04 | 10,232,918.68 | 76.38 | 26,605.42 |
| FSA INTEREST FL | | 0.00 | 0.00 | 95.54 | 0.00 | 0.00 | 0.00 | 0.00 | 2,961.61 | 3,057.15 |
| GREAT WHITE HERON | | 770.40 | 0.00 | 264.95 | 0.00 | 283.24 | 5,181.99 | 3,156,327.77 | 111,182.55 | 117,683.13 |
| HOBE SOUND | | 0.00 | 0.00 | 0.00 | 0.00 | 1,022.20 | 4.28 | 18,000.00 | 8.50 | 1,034.98 |
| ISLAND BAY | | 20.24 | 0.00 | 0.00 | 0.00 | 0.00 | 0.00 | 0.00 | 0.00 | 20.24 |
| J. N. DING DARLING | | 407.02 | 0.00 | 0.00 | 0.00 | 366.20 | 4,458.93 | 8,392,381.50 | 1,174.64 | 6,406.79 |
| KEY WEST | | 1,865.17 CG | 154.00 | 0.00 | 0.00 | 0.00 | 0.00 | 0.00 | 206,289.00 | 208,308.17 |
| LAKE WALES RIDGE | | 0.00 | 0.00 | 0.00 | 0.00 | 0.00 | 1,857.58 | 3,358,500.00 | 0.00 | 1,857.58 |
| LAKE WOODRUFF | | 0.00 | 0.00 | 7.00 | 0.00 | 642.66 | 18,502.36 | 1,404,690.75 | 2,437.00 | 21,559.02 |
| LOWER SUWANNEE | | 0.00 | 0.00 | 0.00 | 0.00 | 75.00 | 49,270.38 | 13,682,080.00 | 1,584.94 | 51,000.32 |
| MATLACHA PASS | | 277.61 | 0.00 | 0.00 | 0.00 | 115.03 | 145.61 | 880,000.00 | 0.00 | 538.25 |
| MERRITT ISLAND | | 0.00 | 0.00 | 0.00 NA | 138,262.70 | 0.00 | 925.70 | 1,335,689.00 | 1.00 | 139,189.40 |
| NATIONAL KEY DEER | | 52.78 | 0.00 | 0.00 | 0.00 | 805.65 | 7,876.30 | 28,216,555.41 | 75,361.61 | 84,096.54 |
| OKEFENOKEE | (1) | 0.00 | 0.00 | 0.00 | 0.00 | 0.00 | 3,678.14 | 52,636.00 | 46.34 | 3,724.48 |
| PASSAGE KEY | | 36.37 | 0.00 | 0.00 | 0.00 | 0.00 | 0.00 | 0.00 | 27.50 | 63.87 |
| PELICAN ISLAND | | 43.00 | 0.00 | 0.00 | 0.00 | 0.00 | 357.99 | 23,018,690.00 | 5,009.45 | 5,410.44 |
| PINE ISLAND | | 175.17 | 0.00 | 0.00 | 0.00 | 0.00 | 427.07 | 2,434,000.00 | 0.00 | 602.24 |
| PINELLAS | | 0.00 | 0.00 | 0.00 | 0.00 | 0.00 | 17.35 | 20,000.00 | 377.00 | 394.35 |
| ST. JOHNS | | 0.00 | 0.00 | 0.00 | 0.00 | 2.50 | 6,254.95 | 2,878,323.64 | 0.00 | 6,257.45 |

TABLE 3 - NATIONAL WILDLIFE REFUGES

| STATE AND UNIT | | RESERVED FROM PUBLIC DOMAIN | | ACQUIRED BY OTHER FEDERAL AGENCY | | DEVISE OR GIFT | PURCHASED | | AGREEMENT EASEMENT OR LEASE | TOTAL ACRES |
|---|---|---|---|---|---|---|---|---|---|---|
| | | SOLE OR PRIMARY | SECONDARY | SOLE OR PRIMARY | SECONDARY | | ACRES | COST ($) | | |
| **FLORIDA** | | | | | | | | | | |
| ST. MARKS | | 91.25 | 0.00 | 31,709.49 | 0.00 | 363.64 | 36,586.13 | 3,943,611.81 | 443.29 | 69,196.75 |
| ST. VINCENT | | 45.33 | 0.00 | 0.00 | 0.00 | 0.00 | 12,444.60 | 2,035,000.00 | 0.00 | 12,489.93 |
| TEN THOUSAND ISLANDS | | 0.00 | 0.00 | 0.00 | 0.00 | 0.00 | 21,543.00 | 0.00 | 13,490.60 | 35,033.60 |
| STATE TOTAL | 29 | 4,853.76 | 154.00 | 32,082.60 | 138,262.70 | 4,436.16 | 236,527.77 | 131,032,804.45 | 562,321.51 | 977,640.50 |
| **GEORGIA** | | | | | | | | | | |
| BANKS LAKE | | 0.00 | 0.00 | 490.00 | 0.00 | 0.00 | 3,069.00 | 356,000.00 | 0.00 | 3,559.00 |
| BLACKBEARD ISLAND | | 0.00 | 0.00 | 4,658.64 | 0.00 | 0.00 | 959.00 | 0.00 | 0.00 | 5,617.64 |
| BOND SWAMP | | 0.00 | 0.00 | 0.00 | 0.00 | 786.24 | 5,490.25 | 2,758,250.00 | 0.00 | 6,276.49 |
| EUFAULA | (15) | 0.00 | 0.00 | 0.00 E | 3,231.00 | 0.00 | 0.00 | 0.00 | 0.00 | 3,231.00 |
| FSA INTEREST GA | ** | 0.00 | 0.00 | 886.38 | 0.00 | 0.00 | 0.00 | 0.00 | 4,053.95 | 4,940.33 |
| HARRIS NECK | | 0.00 | 0.00 | 2,686.94 | 0.00 | 0.00 | 66.41 | 450,000.00 | 70.57 | 2,823.92 |
| OKEFENOKEE | (6) | 0.00 | 0.00 | 1,860.44 | 0.00 | 22,985.54 | 374,137.92 | 1,780,185.12 | 0.00 | 398,983.90 |
| PIEDMONT | | 0.00 | 0.00 | 24,238.22 | 0.00 | 0.00 | 10,717.46 | 44,000.00 | 11.30 | 34,966.98 |
| SAVANNAH | (7) | 0.00 | 0.00 | 4,015.04 | 0.00 | 0.00 | 9,280.17 | 3,321,852.40 | 868.27 | 14,163.48 |
| WASSAW | | 0.00 | 0.00 | 0.00 | 0.00 | 10,049.87 | 0.00 | 0.00 | 3.43 | 10,053.30 |
| WOLF ISLAND | | 0.00 | 0.00 | 538.00 | 0.00 | 0.00 | 4,587.82 | 120,813.52 | 0.00 | 5,125.82 |
| STATE TOTAL | 8 | 0.00 | 0.00 | 39,373.68 | 3,231.00 | 33,021.65 | 408,308.03 | 8,851,101.04 | 5,007.52 | 488,941.86 |
| **HAWAII** | | | | | | | | | | |
| HAKALAU FOREST | | 0.00 | 0.00 | 0.00 | 0.00 | 0.00 | 28,005.12 | 26,178,265.00 | 42.32 | 38,047.44 |
| HANALEI | | 0.00 | 0.00 | 0.00 | 0.00 | 0.00 | 917.42 | 1,289,080.60 | 0.00 | 917.42 |
| HAWAIIAN ISLANDS | | 254,458.10 | 0.00 | 0.00 | 0.00 | 0.00 | 0.00 | 0.00 | 0.00 | 254,458.10 |
| HULEIA | | 0.00 | 0.00 | 0.00 | 0.00 | 0.00 | 240.17 | 327,623.00 | 0.94 | 241.11 |
| JAMES CAMPBELL | | 0.00 | 0.00 | 0.00 | 0.00 | 0.00 | 222.27 | 1,511,498.00 | 37.28 | 259.56 |
| KAKAHAIA | | 0.00 | 0.00 | 0.00 | 0.00 | 0.00 | 44.61 | 684,550.00 | 0.00 | 44.61 |
| KEALIA POND | | 0.00 | 0.00 | 0.00 | 0.00 | 0.00 | 0.00 | 0.00 | 691.56 | 691.56 |
| KILAUEA POINT | | 0.00 | 0.00 | 31.00 | 0.00 | 91.38 | 59.48 | 6,475,000.00 | 16.82 | 198.68 |
| OAHU FOREST | | 0.00 | 0.00 | 0.00 | 0.00 | 0.00 | 4,524.06 | 3,620,000.00 | 44.90 | 4,568.56 |
| PEARL HARBOR | | 0.00 | 0.00 | 37.37 N | 61.15 | 0.00 | 0.00 | 0.00 | 0.00 | 98.52 |
| STATE TOTAL | 10 | 254,458.10 | 0.00 | 68.37 | 61.15 | 91.38 | 44,013.73 | 40,086,004.60 | 833.82 | 299,486.55 |
| **IDAHO** | | | | | | | | | | |
| BEAR LAKE | | 16,977.61 | 0.00 | 0.00 | 0.00 | 0.00 | 1,107.97 | 339,879.30 | 0.00 | 18,085.58 |
| CAMAS | | 0.00 | 0.00 | 0.00 | 0.00 | 0.00 | 10,578.34 | 202,701.84 | 0.00 | 10,578.34 |
| DEER FLAT | (4) | 290.54 R | 9,903.28 | 0.00 | 0.00 | 21.26 | 342.89 | 26,415.50 | 0.00 | 10,547.57 |
| FSA INTEREST ID | ** | 0.00 | 0.00 | 998.60 | 0.00 | 0.00 | 0.00 | 0.00 | 112.00 | 1,110.60 |
| GRAYS LAKE | | 80.00 | 0.00 | 0.00 | 0.00 | 500.00 | 4,463.93 | 2,107,500.00 | 15,421.15 | 20,125.08 |
| KOOTENAI | | 0.00 | 0.00 | 0.00 | 0.00 | 0.00 | 2,774.15 | 708,100.00 | 0.14 | 2,774.29 |
| MINIDOKA | | 1,070.00 R | 17,903.12 | 1,740.00 | 0.00 | 0.00 | 0.00 | 0.00 | 38.64 | 20,751.76 |
| STATE TOTAL | 6 | 18,417.75 | 27,916.40 | 2,738.60 | 0.00 | 181.26 | 19,167.28 | 3,614,196.64 | 15,551.93 | 83,973.22 |
| **ILLINOIS** | | | | | | | | | | |
| CHAUTAUQUA | | 0.00 | 0.00 | 0.00 | 0.00 | 1,706.54 | 4,488.41 | 30,592.80 | 283.61 | 6,480.56 |
| CRAB ORCHARD | | 0.00 | 0.00 | 42,507.58 | 0.00 | 0.00 | 1,401.84 | 486,203.50 | 0.00 | 43,909.42 |
| CYPRESS CREEK | | 0.00 | 0.00 | 0.00 | 0.00 | 1.85 | 15,574.37 | 11,827,237.98 | 0.00 | 15,576.22 |
| EMIQUON | | 0.00 | 0.00 | 0.00 | 0.00 | 0.00 | 2,154.94 | 3,145,400.00 | 0.00 | 2,154.94 |
| FSA INTEREST IL | ** | 0.00 | 0.00 | 335.40 | 0.00 | 0.00 | 0.00 | 0.00 | 0.00 | 335.40 |
| GREAT RIVER | (8) | 0.00 | 0.00 | 0.00 E | 5,490.61 | 59.96 | 1,569.87 | 353,202.72 | 0.00 | 7,110.63 |
| MEREDOSIA | | 0.00 | 0.00 | 0.00 | 0.00 | 2,141.49 | 1,259.31 | 1,328,790.00 | 0.00 | 3,400.80 |
| MIDDLE MISSISSIPPI RIVER | (8) | 0.00 | 0.00 | 0.00 | 0.00 | 903.97 | 2,237.53 | 398,798.00 | 0.00 | 3,141.50 |
| PORT LOUISA | (19) | 0.00 | 0.00 | 0.00 E | 1,466.00 | 0.00 | 4.60 | 11,500.00 | 0.29 | 1,470.89 |
| TWO RIVERS | (8) | 0.00 | 0.00 | 0.00 E | 7,017.00 | 2.31 | 853.17 | 462,343.75 | 160.72 | 8,033.20 |

TABLE 3 - NATIONAL WILDLIFE REFUGES

| STATE AND UNIT | | RESERVED FROM PUBLIC DOMAIN | | ACQUIRED BY OTHER FEDERAL AGENCY | | DEVISE OR GIFT | PURCHASED | | AGREEMENT EASEMENT OR LEASE | TOTAL ACRES |
|---|---|---|---|---|---|---|---|---|---|---|
| | | SOLE OR PRIMARY | SECONDARY | SOLE OR PRIMARY | SECONDARY | | ACRES | COST ($) | | |
| **ILLINOIS** | | | | | | | | | | |
| UPPER MISSISSIPPI RIVER | (9) | 65.15 | 0.00 | 3,344.63 E | 26,956.47 | 0.00 | 2,924.73 | 48,619.98 | 0.99 | 33,291.17 |
| STATE TOTAL | 10 | 65.15 | 0.00 | 46,187.61 | 40,900.28 | 4,818.11 | 32,458.77 | 18,090,685.73 | 444.81 | 124,904.73 |
| **INDIANA** | | | | | | | | | | |
| BIG OAKS | | 0.00 | 0.00 | 0.00 A | 51,000.00 | 0.00 | 0.00 | 0.00 | 0.00 | 55,000.00 |
| FSA INTEREST IN | ** * | 0.00 | 0.00 | 219.03 | 0.00 | 0.00 | 0.00 | 0.00 | 0.00 | 219.03 |
| MUSCATATUCK | | 0.00 | 0.00 | 0.00 | 0.00 | 78.23 | 7,723.99 | 3,612,837.72 | 0.00 | 7,802.22 |
| PATOKA RIVER | | 0.00 | 0.00 | 0.00 | 0.00 | 334.35 | 5,689.82 | 4,792,154.88 | 0.00 | 6,024.17 |
| STATE TOTAL | 3 | 0.00 | 0.00 | 219.03 | 51,000.00 | 412.58 | 13,413.81 | 8,404,992.60 | 0.00 | 69,045.42 |
| **IOWA** | | | | | | | | | | |
| DESOTO | (10) | 0.00 | 0.00 | 0.00 | 0.00 | 0.00 | 3,499.16 | 735,409.28 | 3.61 | 3,502.77 |
| DRIFTLESS AREA | | 0.00 | 0.00 | 0.00 | 0.00 | 0.00 | 811.79 | 463,474.50 | 0.00 | 811.79 |
| NEAL SMITH | | 0.00 | 0.00 | 0.00 | 0.00 | 0.00 | 5,383.03 | 7,867,790.00 | 0.00 | 5,383.03 |
| NO. TALLGRASS PRAIRIE | (47) | 0.00 | 0.00 | 0.00 | 0.00 | 0.00 | 160.00 | 176,000.00 | 0.00 | 160.00 |
| PORT LOUISA | (11) * | 0.00 | 0.00 | 0.00 E | 10,423.94 | 80.00 | 12,119.44 | 2,583,549.54 | 0.00 | 22,623.38 |
| UNION SLOUGH | | 0.00 | 0.00 | 0.00 | 0.00 | 0.00 | 2,845.24 | 210,406.89 | 70.70 | 2,915.94 |
| UPPER MISSISSIPPI RIVER | (10) * | 233.66 | 0.00 | 0.00 E | 30,315.00 | 0.57 | 20,468.95 | 898,867.96 | 0.00 | 55,147.78 |
| STATE TOTAL | 5 | 233.66 | 0.00 | 0.00 | 40,738.94 | 80.57 | 45,317.21 | 13,062,487.97 | 74.31 | 96,544.69 |
| **KANSAS** | | | | | | | | | | |
| FLINT HILLS | | 0.00 | 0.00 | 0.00 E | 18,463.21 | 0.00 | 0.00 | 0.00 | 0.15 | 18,463.36 |
| FSA INTEREST KS | ** * | 0.00 | 0.00 | 116.50 | 0.00 | 0.00 | 0.00 | 0.00 | 0.00 | 116.50 |
| KIRWIN | | 0.00 | 0.00 | 0.00 R | 10,778.00 | 0.00 | 0.00 | 0.00 | 0.00 | 10,778.00 |
| MARAIS DES CYGNES | | 0.00 | 0.00 | 0.00 | 0.00 | 21.00 | 7,341.77 | 3,171,756.80 | 0.00 | 7,364.77 |
| QUIVIRA | | 0.00 | 0.00 | 0.00 | 0.00 | 199.20 | 21,820.10 | 2,059,238.00 | 0.00 | 22,019.30 |
| STATE TOTAL | 4 | 0.00 | 0.00 | 116.50 | 29,241.21 | 222.20 | 29,161.87 | 5,230,994.40 | 0.15 | 58,741.93 |
| **KENTUCKY** | | | | | | | | | | |
| CLARKS RIVER | | 0.00 | 0.00 | 0.00 | 0.00 | 0.00 | 7,914.80 | 7,707,809.00 | 0.00 | 7,914.80 |
| OHIO RIVER ISLANDS | (38) * | 0.00 | 0.00 | 0.00 | 0.00 | 0.00 | 404.56 | 288,640.00 | 0.00 | 404.56 |
| REELFOOT | (14) | 0.00 | 0.00 | 0.00 | 0.00 | 0.00 | 2,039.64 | 418,480.95 | 0.00 | 2,039.64 |
| STATE TOTAL | 2 | 0.00 | 0.00 | 0.00 | 0.00 | 0.00 | 10,359.00 | 8,414,899.95 | 0.00 | 10,359.00 |
| **LOUISIANA** | | | | | | | | | | |
| ATCHAFALAYA | | 0.00 | 0.00 | 0.00 | 0.00 | 0.00 | 15,255.23 | 11,065,658.00 | 0.00 | 15,255.23 |
| BAYOU COCODRIE | | 0.00 | 0.00 | 0.00 | 0.00 | 0.00 | 13,168.51 | 7,816,578.00 | 0.00 | 13,168.51 |
| BAYOU SAUVAGE | | 0.00 | 0.00 | 0.00 | 0.00 | 0.00 | 22,265.12 | 11,010,000.00 | 0.00 | 22,265.12 |
| BAYOU TECHE | | 0.00 | 0.00 | 0.00 | 0.00 | 0.00 | 9,073.50 | 2,234,000.00 | 0.00 | 9,073.50 |
| BIG BRANCH MARSH | | 0.00 | 0.00 | 0.00 | 0.00 | 11,586.54 | 5,780.25 | 9,035,174.00 | 0.00 | 17,366.79 |
| BLACK BAYOU LAKE | | 0.00 | 0.00 | 0.00 | 0.00 | 0.00 | 2,902.31 | 8,074,500.00 | 1,620.00 | 4,522.31 |
| BOGUE CHITTO | (27) | 0.00 | 0.00 | 0.00 | 0.00 | 35.00 | 28,755.79 | 13,438,223.85 | 762.00 | 29,552.79 |
| BRETON | | 9,047.00 | 0.00 | 0.00 | 0.00 | 0.00 | 0.00 | 0.00 | 0.00 | 9,047.00 |
| CAMERON PRAIRIE | | 0.00 | 0.00 | 14,926.73 | 0.00 | 0.00 | 9,621.30 | 5,090,690.00 | 0.00 | 24,548.03 |
| CAT ISLAND | | 0.00 | 0.00 | 0.00 | 0.00 | 13.40 | 9,611.51 | 9,096,572.00 | 0.00 | 9,624.91 |
| CATAHOULA | | 0.00 | 0.00 | 0.00 | 0.00 | 6,272.84 | 14,909.61 | 2,191,497.25 | 3,727.16 | 24,909.61 |
| D'ARBONNE | | 0.00 | 0.00 | 17,419.63 | 0.00 | 0.00 | 0.00 | 0.00 | 0.00 | 17,419.63 |
| DELTA | | 1,407.68 E | 2,892.30 | 10,596.42 | 0.00 | 0.00 | 34,462.73 | 233,324.57 | 0.00 | 48,799.10 |
| FSA INTEREST LA | ** * | 0.00 | 0.00 | 5,729.90 | 0.00 | 0.00 | 0.00 | 0.00 | 5,580.44 | 11,310.34 |
| GRAND COTE | | 0.00 | 0.00 | 0.00 | 0.00 | 0.00 | 5,997.00 | 1,776,000.00 | 80.00 | 6,077.00 |
| HANDY BRAKE | | 0.00 | 0.00 | 465.70 | 0.00 | 0.00 | 0.00 | 0.00 | 35.00 | 500.70 |
| LACASSINE | | 0.00 | 0.00 | 22,991.51 | 0.00 | 0.00 | 10,734.75 | 1,598,296.43 | 652.51 | 34,378.77 |
| LAKE OPHELIA | | 0.00 | 0.00 | 53.70 | 0.00 | 0.00 | 17,347.76 | 7,302,080.00 | 200.00 | 17,561.46 |
| MANDALAY | | 0.00 | 0.00 | 0.00 | 0.00 | 4,416.00 | 0.00 | 0.00 | 203.00 | 4,619.00 |

TABLE 3 - NATIONAL WILDLIFE REFUGES

| STATE AND UNIT | RESERVED FROM PUBLIC DOMAIN | | ACQUIRED BY OTHER FEDERAL AGENCY | | DEVISE OR GIFT | PURCHASED | | AGREEMENT EASEMENT OR LEASE | TOTAL ACRES |
|---|---|---|---|---|---|---|---|---|---|
| | SOLE OR PRIMARY | SECONDARY | SOLE OR PRIMARY | SECONDARY | | ACRES | COST ($) | | |
| **LOUISIANA** | | | | | | | | | |
| RED RIVER | 0.00 | 0.00 | 0.00 | 0.00 | 0.00 | 7,701.13 | 7,536,832.00 | 1,122.86 | 8,823.99 |
| SABINE | 0.00 | 0.00 | 123,943.42 | 0.00 | 0.00 | 566.66 | 14,000.51 | 1,280.00 | 125,790.08 |
| SHELL KEYS | 8.00 | 0.00 | 0.00 | 0.00 | 0.00 | 0.00 | 0.00 | 0.00 | 8.00 |
| TENSAS RIVER | 0.00 | 0.00 | 53,174.58 | 0.00 | 528.85 | 17,297.17 | 13,309,410.00 | 195.17 | 71,193.77 |
| UPPER OUACHITA | 0.00 | 0.00 | 0.00 | 0.00 | 0.00 | 42,524.59 | 21,312,800.00 | 3,240.95 | 46,065.49 |
| STATE TOTAL 23 | 10,462.65 | 2,892.30 | 248,721.59 | 0.00 | 22,850.63 | 268,294.91 | 129,201,678.21 | 18,679.05 | 571,861.13 |
| **MAINE** | | | | | | | | | |
| AROOSTOOK | 0.00 | 0.00 | 4,999.22 | 0.00 | 0.00 | 253.03 | 62,120.00 | 0.00 | 5,252.25 |
| CROSS ISLAND | 0.00 | 0.00 | 0.00 | 0.00 | 1,538.40 | 164.70 | 0.00 | 0.00 | 1,703.10 |
| FRANKLIN ISLAND | 0.00 | 0.00 | 11.94 | 0.00 | 0.00 | 0.00 | 0.00 | 0.00 | 11.94 |
| FSA INTEREST ME | 0.00 | 0.00 | 394.08 | 0.00 | 0.00 | 0.00 | 0.00 | 208.00 | 622.08 |
| LAKE UMBAGOG (36) | 0.00 | 0.00 | 0.00 | 0.00 | 24.32 | 5,620.90 | 6,586,474.70 | 0.03 | 5,645.25 |
| MOOSEHORN | 0.00 | 0.00 | 6,490.33 | 0.00 | 332.64 | 21,971.57 | 5,551,107.19 | 80.32 | 28,874.86 |
| PETIT MANAN | 0.00 | 0.00 | 197.02 | 0.00 | 1,727.47 | 3,753.99 | 6,160,694.00 | 285.12 | 5,873.60 |
| POND ISLAND | 0.00 | 0.00 | 50.00 | 0.00 | 0.00 | 0.00 | 0.00 | 0.00 | 10.00 |
| RACHEL CARSON | 0.00 | 0.00 | 0.00 | 0.00 | 598.18 | 4,554.56 | 20,620,806.75 | 172.66 | 5,325.40 |
| SEAL ISLAND | 0.00 | 0.00 | 65.00 | 0.00 | 0.00 | 0.00 | 0.00 | 0.00 | 65.00 |
| SUNKHAZE MEADOWS | 0.00 | 0.00 | 0.00 | 0.00 | 126.30 | 11,090.41 | 2,458,950.00 | 0.00 | 11,216.71 |
| STATE TOTAL 9 | 0.00 | 0.00 | 12,077.59 | 0.00 | 4,347.51 | 47,408.76 | 40,460,152.64 | 766.13 | 64,599.99 |
| **MARYLAND** | | | | | | | | | |
| BLACKWATER | 0.00 | 0.00 | 0.00 | 0.00 | 1,370.73 | 24,354.77 | 13,704,344.01 | 0.00 | 25,685.50 |
| CHINCOTEAGUE (16) | 0.00 | 0.00 | 0.00 | 0.00 | 0.00 | 417.81 | 13,780.42 | 0.00 | 417.81 |
| EASTERN NECK | 0.00 | 0.00 | 0.00 | 0.00 | 0.00 | 2,286.27 | 1,606,145.09 | 0.00 | 2,286.27 |
| FSA INTEREST MD | 0.00 | 0.00 | 0.00 | 0.00 | 0.00 | 0.00 | 0.00 | 87.94 | 87.94 |
| MARTIN (16) | 0.00 | 0.00 | 0.00 | 0.00 | 2,560.80 | 1,863.57 | 61,027.06 | 0.00 | 4,423.43 |
| PATUXENT | 0.00 | 0.00 | 11,852.10 | 0.00 | 0.00 | 988.83 | 1,310,786.71 | 0.27 | 12,841.20 |
| SUSQUEHANNA | 0.00 | 0.00 | 3.79 | 0.00 | 0.00 | 0.00 | 0.00 | 0.00 | 3.79 |
| STATE TOTAL 5 | 0.00 | 0.00 | 11,855.89 | 0.00 | 3,940.59 | 29,861.25 | 16,696,083.23 | 68.21 | 45,725.94 |
| **MASSACHUSETTS** | | | | | | | | | |
| ASSABET RIVER | 0.00 | 0.00 | 2,229.20 | 0.00 | 0.00 | 0.00 | 0.00 | 0.00 | 2,229.20 |
| GREAT MEADOWS | 0.00 | 0.00 | 0.00 | 0.00 | 284.53 | 3,547.95 | 11,854,900.90 | 17.33 | 3,849.81 |
| MASHPEE | 0.00 | 0.00 | 0.00 | 0.00 | 3.00 | 284.40 | 2,810,000.00 | 54.25 | 341.65 |
| MASSASOIT | 0.00 | 0.00 | 0.00 | 0.00 | 0.00 | 208.51 | 1,142,332.00 | 0.00 | 208.51 |
| MONOMOY | 0.00 | 0.00 | 2.10 | 0.00 | 0.00 | 7,601.90 | 549,465.00 | 0.00 | 7,604.00 |
| NANTUCKET | 0.00 | 0.00 | 24.00 | 0.00 | 0.00 | 0.00 | 0.00 | 0.00 | 24.00 |
| NOMANS LAND ISLAND | 0.00 | 0.00 | 628.00 | 0.00 | 0.00 | 0.00 | 0.00 | 0.00 | 628.00 |
| OXBOW | 0.00 | 0.00 | 1,547.33 | 0.00 | 4.29 | 125.40 | 3,410,000.00 | 0.00 | 1,677.02 |
| PARKER RIVER | 0.00 | 0.00 | 1.90 | 0.00 | 0.00 | 4,650.61 | 537,740.84 | 0.00 | 4,652.51 |
| SILVIO O. CONTE (42) | 0.00 | 0.00 | 0.00 | 0.00 | 3.80 | 234.63 | 2,887,210.00 | 0.00 | 238.43 |
| THACHER ISLAND | 0.00 | 0.00 | 22.00 | 0.00 | 0.00 | 0.00 | 0.00 | 0.00 | 22.00 |
| STATE TOTAL 10 | 0.00 | 0.00 | 4,454.53 | 0.00 | 295.62 | 16,663.40 | 22,791,648.74 | 71.58 | 21,475.93 |
| **MICHIGAN** | | | | | | | | | |
| DETROIT RIVER | 304.47 | 0.00 | 168.00 | 0.00 | 32.51 | 562.03 | 4,730,000.00 | 3,143.95 | 4,210.96 |
| FSA INTEREST MI | 0.00 | 0.00 | 94.00 | 0.00 | 0.00 | 0.00 | 0.00 | 0.00 | 94.00 |
| HARBOR ISLAND | 0.00 | 0.00 | 0.00 | 0.00 | 0.00 | 695.00 | 197,000.00 | 0.00 | 695.00 |
| HURON | 22.50 | 0.00 | 124.35 | 0.00 | 0.00 | 0.00 | 0.00 | 0.00 | 146.85 |
| KIRTLANDS WARBLER | 0.00 | 0.00 | 0.00 | 0.00 | 0.00 | 6,684.46 | 3,528,886.46 | 0.00 | 6,684.46 |
| MICHIGAN ISLANDS | 11.94 CG | 121.70 | 229.70 | 0.00 | 234.05 | 0.00 | 0.00 | 0.00 | 597.39 |
| SENEY | 2,860.40 | 0.00 | 7,068.99 | 0.02 | 0.00 | 85,525.62 | 177,178.96 | 0.00 | 95,244.81 |

TABLE 3 - NATIONAL WILDLIFE REFUGES

| STATE AND UNIT | | RESERVED FROM PUBLIC DOMAIN | | ACQUIRED BY OTHER FEDERAL AGENCY | | DEVISE OR GIFT | PURCHASED | | AGREEMENT EASEMENT OR LEASE | TOTAL ACRES |
|---|---|---|---|---|---|---|---|---|---|---|
| | | SOLE OR PRIMARY | SECONDARY | SOLE OR PRIMARY | SECONDARY | | ACRES | COST ($) | | |
| **MICHIGAN** | | | | | | | | | | |
| SHIAWASSEE | | 0.00 | 0.00 | 0.00 | 0.00 | 52.21 | 8,960.54 | 2,470,375.87 | 300.00 | 9,362.75 |
| STATE TOTAL | 7 | 2,999.51 | 121.70 | 7,674.64 | 0.00 | 318.77 | 102,427.65 | 11,101,441.02 | 3,490.95 | 117,006.22 |
| **MINNESOTA** | | | | | | | | | | |
| AGASSIZ | | 0.00 | 0.00 | 60,091.98 | 0.00 | 0.00 | 954.33 | 40,225.96 | 446.75 | 61,500.83 |
| BIG STONE | | 0.00 | 0.00 | 10,540.43 E | 254.20 | 0.00 | 790.79 | 779,900.00 | 0.00 | 11,585.42 |
| CRANE MEADOWS | | 0.00 | 0.00 | 0.00 | 0.00 | 60.00 | 1,694.17 | 1,156,965.00 | 0.00 | 1,754.17 |
| FSA INTEREST MN | ** | 0.00 | 0.00 | 3,326.80 | 0.00 | 0.00 | 0.00 | 0.00 | 0.00 | 3,326.80 |
| GLACIAL RIDGE | | 0.00 | 0.00 | 0.00 | 0.00 | 2,306.00 | 54.02 | 255,000.00 | 0.00 | 2,360.02 |
| HAMDEN SLOUGH | | 0.00 | 0.00 | 0.00 | 0.00 | 0.00 | 3,136.45 | 1,832,872.00 | 71.40 | 3,209.85 |
| MILLE LACS | | 0.00 | 0.00 | 0.00 | 0.00 | 0.00 | 0.00 | 0.00 | 0.00 | 0.60 |
| MINNESOTA VALLEY | | 0.00 | 0.00 | 364.98 | 0.00 | 1,300.51 | 7,369.85 | 19,965,653.83 | 1,701.18 | 10,736.52 |
| NO. TALLGRASS PRAIRIE | (19) | 0.00 | 0.00 | 0.00 | 0.00 | 0.00 | 2,133.12 | 2,480,675.00 | 1,938.47 | 4,071.59 |
| RICE LAKE | | 0.00 | 0.00 | 9,831.57 | 0.00 | 0.00 | 6,640.71 | 265,329.77 | 0.00 | 16,472.28 |
| RYDELL | | 0.00 | 0.00 | 0.00 | 0.00 | 2,070.00 | 0.00 | 0.00 | 0.00 | 2,070.00 |
| SHERBURNE | | 0.00 | 0.00 | 0.00 | 0.00 | 0.00 | 29,677.84 | 3,296,341.05 | 0.00 | 29,677.84 |
| TAMARAC | | 40.00 | 0.00 | 0.00 | 0.00 | 0.00 | 35,151.38 | 612,159.30 | 0.00 | 35,191.38 |
| UPPER MISSISSIPPI RIVER | (18) | 241.58 | 0.00 | 0.00 E | 15,420.77 | 193.45 | 17,832.46 | 480,904.80 | 92.97 | 33,781.23 |
| STATE TOTAL | 11 | 288.18 | 0.00 | 84,155.66 | 15,674.97 | 5,932.96 | 105,432.09 | 31,167,427.22 | 4,254.77 | 215,738.63 |
| **MISSISSIPPI** | | | | | | | | | | |
| BOGUE CHITTO | (28) | 0.00 | 0.00 | 0.00 | 0.00 | 0.00 | 6,949.08 | 6,495,784.00 | 0.00 | 6,949.08 |
| COLDWATER RIVER | | 0.00 | 0.00 | 94.28 | 0.00 | 0.00 | 2,374.10 | 1,430,450.00 | 0.00 | 2,468.38 |
| DAHOMEY | | 0.00 | 0.00 | 0.00 | 0.00 | 162.00 | 8,744.80 | 4,900,000.00 | 260.00 | 9,166.80 |
| FSA INTEREST MS | ** | 0.00 | 0.00 | 11,758.00 | 0.00 | 0.00 | 0.00 | 0.00 | 6,940.71 | 18,698.71 |
| GRAND BAY | (5) | 0.00 | 0.00 | 0.00 | 0.00 | 4,456.63 | 2,964.86 | 2,719,643.00 | 0.00 | 7,421.49 |
| HILLSIDE | | 0.00 | 0.00 | 15,383.53 | 0.00 | 22.74 | 3,645.52 | 2,879,900.00 | 0.00 | 19,051.39 |
| HOLT COLLIER | | 0.00 | 0.00 | 1,359.35 | 0.00 | 0.00 | 80.34 | 68,300.00 | 0.00 | 1,439.69 |
| MATHEWS BRAKE | | 0.00 | 0.00 | 0.00 | 0.00 | 0.00 | 2,414.71 | 1,691,446.00 | 0.00 | 2,414.71 |
| MISSISSIPPI SANDHILL CRANE | | 0.00 | 0.00 | 0.00 | 0.00 | 157.78 | 18,001.50 | 21,715,501.00 | 1,679.28 | 19,838.56 |
| MORGAN BRAKE | | 0.00 | 0.00 | 0.00 | 0.00 | 131.83 | 7,241.28 | 4,517,662.20 | 0.00 | 7,373.11 |
| NOXUBEE | | 40.08 | 0.00 | 35,343.85 | 0.00 | 80.00 | 11,688.36 | 145,414.06 | 0.00 | 47,152.29 |
| PANTHER SWAMP | | 0.00 | 0.00 | 0.00 E | 7,070.45 | 0.00 | 28,249.29 | 15,045,723.00 | 641.51 | 35,961.25 |
| ST. CATHERINE CREEK | | 0.00 | 0.00 | 0.00 | 0.00 | 0.00 | 24,429.29 | 12,825,167.00 | 502.10 | 24,931.39 |
| TALLAHATCHIE | | 0.00 | 0.00 | 0.00 | 0.00 | 0.00 | 2,324.14 | 1,361,000.00 | 470.00 | 2,794.14 |
| THEODORE ROOSEVELT | | 0.00 | 0.00 | 6,698.82 | 0.00 | 0.00 | 0.00 | 0.00 | 0.00 | 6,698.82 |
| YAZOO | | 0.00 | 0.00 | 0.00 | 0.00 | 0.00 | 12,942.64 | 2,692,503.78 | 0.00 | 12,942.64 |
| STATE TOTAL | 13 | 40.08 | 0.00 | 70,627.41 | 7,070.45 | 5,010.98 | 132,049.91 | 78,157,514.03 | 10,460.66 | 225,250.43 |
| **MISSOURI** | | | | | | | | | | |
| BIG MUDDY | | 0.00 | 0.00 | 442.00 A | 5,300.00 | 31.67 | 9,260.29 | 7,116,000.00 | 1.68 | 11,035.64 |
| CLARENCE CANNON | | 0.00 | 0.00 | 0.00 | 0.00 | 0.00 | 3,749.98 | 1,175,364.25 | 0.00 | 3,749.98 |
| FSA INTEREST MO | ** | 0.00 | 0.00 | 1,673.06 | 0.00 | 0.00 | 0.00 | 0.00 | 111.62 | 1,784.68 |
| GREAT RIVER | (11) | 0.00 | 0.00 | 0.00 | 0.00 | 0.00 | 2,108.43 | 1,008,000.00 | 0.00 | 2,108.43 |
| MIDDLE MISSISSIPPI RIVER | (15) | 0.00 | 0.00 | 0.00 | 0.00 | 0.00 | 1,704.17 | 1,914,825.00 | 0.00 | 1,704.17 |
| MINGO | | 0.00 | 0.00 | 0.00 | 0.00 | 0.00 | 21,591.25 | 317,365.82 | 69.80 | 21,661.05 |
| OZARK CAVEFISH | | 0.00 | 0.00 | 0.00 | 0.00 | 0.00 | 41.80 | 132,000.00 | 0.00 | 41.80 |
| PILOT KNOB | | 0.00 | 0.00 | 0.00 | 0.00 | 90.00 | 0.00 | 0.00 | 0.00 | 90.00 |
| SQUAW CREEK | | 0.00 | 0.00 | 3,049.10 | 0.00 | 0.00 | 4,300.96 | 573,971.89 | 64.83 | 7,414.89 |
| SWAN LAKE | | 0.00 | 0.00 | 5,923.42 | 0.00 | 0.00 | 5,569.55 | 355,103.19 | 0.00 | 11,492.97 |
| TWO RIVERS | (11) | 0.00 | 0.00 | 0.00 E | 232.00 | 0.00 | 0.00 | 0.00 | 0.00 | 232.00 |
| STATE TOTAL | 7 | 0.00 | 0.00 | 11,087.58 | 1,532.00 | 121.67 | 48,326.43 | 12,592,703.15 | 247.93 | 61,315.61 |

TABLE 3 - NATIONAL WILDLIFE REFUGES

| STATE AND UNIT | RESERVED FROM PUBLIC DOMAIN | | ACQUIRED BY OTHER FEDERAL AGENCY | | DEVISE OR GIFT | PURCHASED | | AGREEMENT EASEMENT OR LEASE | TOTAL ACRES |
| | SOLE OR PRIMARY | SECONDARY | SOLE OR PRIMARY | SECONDARY | | ACRES | COST ($) | | |
|---|---|---|---|---|---|---|---|---|---|
| **MONTANA** | | | | | | | | | |
| BENTON LAKE | 12,234.92 | 0.00 | 0.00 | 0.00 | 0.00 | 147.64 | 5,315.00 | 76.88 | 12,459.44 |
| BLACK COULEE | 640.00 | 0.00 | 0.00 | 0.00 | 0.00 | 0.00 | 0.00 | 668.88 | 1,308.88 |
| BLACKFOOT VALLEY | 0.00 | 0.00 | 0.00 | 0.00 | 0.00 | 0.00 | 0.00 | 19,222.64 | 19,222.64 |
| BOWDOIN | 14,796.58 | 0.00 | 640.00 | 0.00 | 0.00 | 0.00 | 0.00 | 515.39 | 15,951.97 |
| CHARLES M. RUSSELL | 358,198.42 E | 380,905.03 | 6,574.02 E | 547,399.11 | 139.37 | 13,577.77 | 3,602,740.00 | 6,876.50 | 915,264.22 |
| CREEDMAN COULEE | 80.00 | 0.00 | 0.00 | 0.00 | 0.00 | 0.00 | 0.00 | 2,648.00 | 2,728.00 |
| FSA INTEREST MT | 0.00 | 0.00 | 270.62 | 0.00 | 0.00 | 0.00 | 0.00 | 1,480.00 | 1,750.62 |
| HAILSTONE | 0.00 | 180.00 | 0.00 | 0.00 | 0.00 | 0.00 | 0.00 | 740.00 | 920.00 |
| HALFBREED LAKE | 0.00 | 0.00 | 0.00 | 0.00 | 0.00 | 3,279.02 | 291,000.00 | 1,039.22 | 4,318.24 |
| HEWITT LAKE | 0.00 | 400.00 | 320.49 | 0.00 | 0.00 | 0.00 | 0.00 | 640.43 | 1,360.92 |
| LAKE MASON | 17.59 | 0.00 | 6,981.65 | 0.00 | 0.00 | 4,256.60 | 18,500.00 | 5,558.68 | 16,814.52 |
| LAKE THIBADEAU | 19.42 | 0.00 | 0.00 | 0.00 | 0.00 | 0.00 | 0.00 | 1,849.06 | 1,868.48 |
| LAMESTEER | 0.00 | 0.00 | 0.00 | 0.00 | 0.00 | 0.00 | 0.00 | 800.00 | 800.00 |
| LEE METCALF | 0.00 | 0.00 | 0.00 | 0.00 | 0.00 | 2,792.52 | 868,080.00 | 0.00 | 2,792.52 |
| LOST TRAIL | 0.00 | 0.00 | 0.00 | 0.00 | 3,112.00 | 4,690.20 | 1,728,205.00 | 1,029.04 | 8,834.24 |
| MEDICINE LAKE | 1,500.99 | 0.00 | 27,412.53 | 0.00 | 3.64 | 2,562.96 | 29,690.00 | 33.59 | 31,503.71 |
| NATIONAL BISON RANGE | 0.00 | 0.00 | 18,475.50 | 0.00 | 0.00 | 320.34 | 477,200.00 | 0.00 | 18,795.84 |
| NINE-PIPE | 0.00 | 0.00 | 0.00 | 0.00 | 0.00 | 0.00 | 0.00 | 4,027.68 | 4,027.68 |
| PABLO | 0.00 | 0.00 | 0.00 | 0.00 | 0.00 | 0.00 | 0.00 | 2,473.52 | 2,473.52 |
| RED ROCK LAKES | 9,218.31 F | 504.28 | 29,483.58 | 0.00 | 340.00 | 5,961.54 | 2,608,856.00 | 20,212.54 | 65,890.25 |
| ROCKY MOUNTAIN FRONT | 0.00 | 0.00 | 0.00 | 0.00 | 0.00 | 0.00 | 0.00 | 4,176.76 | 4,176.76 |
| SWAN RIVER | 0.00 | 0.00 | 0.00 | 0.00 | 0.00 | 1,568.81 | 901,645.00 | 0.00 | 1,568.81 |
| UL BEND | 29,678.22 E | 6,807.46 | 1,298.79 E | 7,825.95 | 0.00 | 9,688.19 | 577,280.00 | 560.00 | 56,049.56 |
| WAR HORSE | 0.00 | 0.00 | 3,434.88 | 0.00 | 0.00 | 397.94 | 5.50 | 560.00 | 3,392.87 |
| STATE TOTAL | 23 | 426,432.45 | 388,952.77 | 95,897.09 | 156,325.01 | 3,595.01 | 48,846.58 | 11,158,484.00 | 78,806.81 | 1,195,827.69 |
| **NEBRASKA** | | | | | | | | | |
| BOYER CHUTE | 0.00 | 0.00 | 0.00 | 0.00 | 2,644.49 | 1,395.32 | 3,292,174.92 | 0.00 | 4,039.81 |
| CRESCENT LAKE | 286.87 | 0.00 | 240.00 | 0.00 | 0.00 | 45,457.99 | 323,115.00 | 31.49 | 45,865.35 |
| DESOTO | (19) | 0.00 | 0.00 | 0.00 | 0.00 | 0.00 | 4,324.20 | 761,275.20 | 0.00 | 4,324.20 |
| FORT NIOBRARA | 14,778.12 | 0.00 | 2,383.91 | 0.00 | 76.58 | 1,893.92 | 34,309.32 | 0.00 | 19,132.53 |
| FSA INTEREST NE | 0.00 | 0.00 | 683.70 | 0.00 | 0.00 | 0.00 | 0.00 | 1,645.22 | 2,328.92 |
| JOHN W. & LOUISE SEIER | 0.00 | 0.00 | 0.00 | 0.00 | 2,400.00 | 0.00 | 0.00 | 0.00 | 2,400.00 |
| KARL E. MUNDT | (20) | 0.00 | 0.00 | 0.00 | 0.00 | 19.39 | 0.00 | 0.00 | 0.00 | 19.39 |
| NORTH PLATTE | 742.89 R | 2,684.81 | 0.00 | 0.00 | 0.00 | 45.53 | 27,500.00 | 0.00 | 3,473.23 |
| VALENTINE | 0.00 | 0.00 | 65,114.00 | 0.00 | 60.00 | 6,599.84 | 79,572.00 | 1,324.25 | 73,098.09 |
| STATE TOTAL | 6 | 15,796.88 | 2,684.81 | 68,421.61 | 0.00 | 5,200.46 | 59,716.80 | 4,506,948.44 | 3,000.96 | 134,811.52 |
| **NEVADA** | | | | | | | | | |
| ANAHO ISLAND | 247.73 | 0.00 | 0.00 | 0.00 | 0.00 | 0.00 | 0.00 | 0.00 | 247.73 |
| ASH MEADOWS | 0.00 | 0.00 | 0.00 | 0.00 | 0.00 | 13,485.94 | 6,602,225.00 | 0.00 | 13,485.94 |
| DESERT | 1,614,553.49 | 0.00 | 4.45 | 0.00 | 3.45 | 760.00 | 582,800.00 | 0.00 | 1,615,321.39 |
| FALLON | 0.00 R | 17,901.94 | 0.00 | 0.00 | 0.00 | 0.00 | 0.00 | 0.00 | 17,901.94 |
| MOAPA VALLEY | 0.00 | 0.00 | 0.00 | 0.00 | 0.00 | 115.93 | 3,325,000.00 | 0.00 | 115.93 |
| PAHRANAGAT | 1,466.39 | 0.00 | 0.00 | 0.00 | 0.00 | 3,915.60 | 500,000.00 | 0.75 | 5,382.74 |
| RUBY LAKE | 7,565.53 LM | 120.00 | 0.00 | 0.00 | 0.00 | 31,800.57 | 208,437.25 | 0.00 | 39,286.10 |
| SHELDON | (4) | 544,276.82 LM | 80.00 | 0.00 | 0.00 | 4,775.66 | 23,743.67 | 2,002.00 | 0.00 | 572,876.15 |
| STILLWATER | 76,799.00 | 0.00 | 0.00 | 0.00 | 0.00 | 10,480.37 | 14,006,584.00 | 26.41 | 87,305.78 |
| STATE TOTAL | 9 | 2,244,908.96 | 18,101.94 | 4.45 | 0.00 | 4,779.11 | 84,102.08 | 25,437,048.25 | 27.16 | 2,351,923.70 |
| **NEW HAMPSHIRE** | | | | | | | | | |
| GREAT BAY | 0.00 | 0.00 | 1,054.00 | 0.00 | 0.00 | 33.18 | 1,268,560.00 | 28.90 | 1,116.08 |

TABLE 3 - NATIONAL WILDLIFE REFUGES

| STATE AND UNIT | RESERVED FROM PUBLIC DOMAIN | | ACQUIRED BY OTHER FEDERAL AGENCY | | DEVISE OR GIFT | PURCHASED | | AGREEMENT EASEMENT OR LEASE | TOTAL ACRES |
|---|---|---|---|---|---|---|---|---|---|
| | SOLE OR PRIMARY | SECONDARY | SOLE OR PRIMARY | SECONDARY | | ACRES | COST ($) | | |
| **NEW HAMPSHIRE** | | | | | | | | | |
| JOHN HAY | 0.00 | 0.00 | 0.00 | 0.00 | 164.60 | 0.00 | 0.00 | 0.30 | 164.90 |
| LAKE UMBAGOG (37) | 0.00 | 0.00 | 0.00 | 0.00 | 0.00 | 13,167.48 | 11,341,748.00 | 6.01 | 13,173.49 |
| SILVIO O. CONTE (43) | 0.00 | 0.00 | 0.00 | 0.00 | 0.00 | 5,170.33 | 1,957,972.96 | 168.00 | 5,338.33 |
| WAPACK | 0.00 | 0.00 | 0.00 | 0.00 | 1,672.00 | 0.00 | 0.00 | 0.00 | 1,672.00 |
| STATE TOTAL 4 | 0.00 | 0.00 | 1,054.00 | 0.00 | 1,836.60 | 18,370.99 | 14,596,218.99 | 201.21 | 21,462.80 |
| **NEW JERSEY** | | | | | | | | | |
| CAPE MAY | 0.00 | 0.00 | 0.00 | 0.00 | 0.00 | 10,657.70 | 26,069,013.22 | 490.80 | 11,148.50 |
| EDWIN B. FORSYTHE | 0.00 | 0.00 | 0.00 | 0.00 | 1,388.55 | 42,559.85 | 46,564,809.83 | 2,541.10 | 46,489.50 |
| GREAT SWAMP | 0.00 | 0.00 | 0.00 | 0.00 | 2,872.20 | 4,755.39 | 22,880,308.05 | 29.86 | 7,657.45 |
| SUPAWNA MEADOWS | 0.00 | 0.00 | 6.86 C | 1.96 | 121.00 | 2,885.93 | 1,297,644.00 | 0.00 | 3,015.75 |
| WALLKILL RIVER (39) | 0.00 | 0.00 | 0.00 | 0.00 | 129.65 | 4,829.48 | 20,931,602.50 | 0.00 | 4,959.13 |
| STATE TOTAL 4 | 0.00 | 0.00 | 6.86 | 1.96 | 4,511.40 | 65,688.35 | 117,733,377.60 | 3,061.76 | 73,270.33 |
| **NEW MEXICO** | | | | | | | | | |
| BITTER LAKE | 12,395.71 | 0.00 | 0.00 | 0.00 | 0.00 | 12,212.93 | 843,804.00 | 0.00 | 24,608.64 |
| BOSQUE DEL APACHE | 140.00 | 0.00 | 0.00 | 0.00 | 0.00 | 56,850.31 | 125,311.00 | 200.79 | 57,191.10 |
| GRULLA (12) | 3,230.55 | 0.00 | 0.00 | 0.00 | 0.00 | 0.00 | 0.00 | 0.00 | 3,230.55 |
| LAS VEGAS | 0.00 | 0.00 | 0.00 | 0.00 | 0.00 | 8,672.08 | 2,121,150.00 | 0.00 | 8,672.08 |
| MAXWELL | 0.00 | 0.00 | 0.00 R | 438.52 | 0.00 | 2,791.69 | 423,370.79 | 468.38 | 3,698.59 |
| SAN ANDRES | 0.00 LM | 57,215.48 | 0.00 | 0.00 | 0.00 | 0.00 | 0.00 | 0.00 | 57,215.48 |
| SEVILLETA | 0.00 | 0.00 | 0.00 | 0.00 | 220,200.00 | 9,411.07 | 1,545,765.00 | 62.50 | 229,673.57 |
| STATE TOTAL 7 | 15,766.26 | 57,215.48 | 0.00 | 438.52 | 220,200.00 | 89,938.08 | 5,059,400.79 | 731.67 | 384,290.01 |
| **NEW YORK** | | | | | | | | | |
| AMAGANSETT | 0.00 | 0.00 | 35.84 | 0.00 | 0.00 | 0.00 | 0.00 | 0.00 | 35.84 |
| CONSCIENCE POINT | 0.00 | 0.00 | 0.00 | 0.00 | 60.40 | 0.00 | 0.00 | 0.00 | 60.40 |
| ELIZABETH A. MORTON | 0.00 | 0.00 | 0.00 | 0.00 | 187.19 | 0.00 | 0.00 | 0.00 | 187.19 |
| FSA INTEREST NY ** | 0.00 | 0.00 | 1,178.45 | 0.00 | 0.00 | 0.00 | 0.00 | 1,535.65 | 2,714.10 |
| IROQUOIS | 0.00 | 0.00 | 0.00 | 0.00 | 0.00 | 10,824.61 | 1,281,619.86 | 3.45 | 10,828.06 |
| MONTEZUMA | 0.00 | 0.00 | 0.00 | 0.00 | 12.31 | 8,140.80 | 2,795,050.01 | 409.51 | 8,562.62 |
| OYSTER BAY | 0.00 | 0.00 | 0.00 | 0.00 | 3,204.08 | 0.00 | 0.00 | 0.00 | 3,204.08 |
| SEATUCK | 0.00 | 0.00 | 0.00 | 0.00 | 209.23 | 0.00 | 0.00 | 0.00 | 209.23 |
| SHAWANGUNK GRASSLANDS | 0.00 | 0.00 | 566.53 | 0.00 | 0.00 | 0.00 | 0.00 | 0.00 | 566.53 |
| TARGET ROCK | 0.00 | 0.00 | 0.00 | 0.00 | 80.09 | 0.00 | 0.00 | 0.00 | 80.09 |
| WALLKILL RIVER (40) | 0.00 | 0.00 | 0.00 | 0.00 | 0.00 | 147.09 | 236,960.00 | 0.00 | 147.09 |
| WERTHEIM | 0.00 | 0.00 | 25.96 | 0.00 | 1,870.74 | 674.89 | 6,982,489.80 | 0.00 | 2,571.58 |
| STATE TOTAL 11 | 0.00 | 0.00 | 1,806.77 | 0.00 | 5,624.04 | 19,787.39 | 11,256,319.67 | 1,948.61 | 29,166.81 |
| **NORTH CAROLINA** | | | | | | | | | |
| ALLIGATOR RIVER | 0.00 | 0.00 | 0.00 | 0.00 | 125,360.00 | 27,556.15 | 6,383,287.00 | 0.00 | 152,917.15 |
| CEDAR ISLAND | 0.00 | 0.00 | 31.40 | 0.00 | 1,966.15 | 12,464.77 | 347,171.21 | 0.00 | 14,462.32 |
| CURRITUCK | 0.00 | 0.00 | 0.00 | 0.00 | 0.00 | 4,382.88 | 9,020,384.00 | 1,930.76 | 8,313.64 |
| FSA INTEREST NC ** | 0.00 | 0.00 | 566.49 | 0.00 | 0.00 | 0.00 | 0.00 | 6,055.56 | 6,621.05 |
| GREAT DISMAL SWAMP (15) | 0.00 | 0.00 | 0.00 | 0.00 | 10,957.00 | 15,152.70 | 5,692,564.47 | 0.00 | 26,109.70 |
| MACKAY ISLAND (16) | 0.00 | 0.00 | 0.00 | 0.00 | 841.88 | 6,504.35 | 1,620,306.95 | 0.00 | 7,346.23 |
| MATTAMUSKEET | 0.00 | 0.00 | 49,925.05 | 0.00 | 0.00 | 252.04 | 1,285.35 | 3.09 | 50,180.18 |
| PEA ISLAND | 0.00 | 0.00 | 34.85 CG | 11.38 | 0.00 | 5,787.97 | 40,401.86 | 0.00 | 5,834.20 |
| PEE DEE | 0.00 | 0.00 | 0.00 | 0.00 | 0.00 | 8,438.94 | 2,561,851.76 | 0.00 | 8,438.94 |
| POCOSIN LAKES | 0.00 | 0.00 | 0.00 | 0.00 | 97,756.29 | 12,350.35 | 1,682,157.99 | 0.00 | 110,106.64 |
| ROANOKE RIVER | 0.00 | 0.00 | 0.00 | 0.00 | 0.00 | 21,062.43 | 11,006,258.00 | 0.00 | 21,062.43 |
| SWANQUARTER | 0.00 | 0.00 | 0.00 | 0.00 | 910.33 | 15,500.76 | 61,000.90 | 0.00 | 16,411.09 |
| STATE TOTAL 11 | 0.00 | 0.00 | 50,556.79 | 11.38 | 237,790.65 | 129,475.34 | 38,311,639.52 | 9,989.41 | 427,823.57 |

TABLE 3 - NATIONAL WILDLIFE REFUGES

| STATE AND UNIT | RESERVED FROM PUBLIC DOMAIN | | ACQUIRED BY OTHER FEDERAL AGENCY | | DEVISE OR GIFT | PURCHASED | | AGREEMENT EASEMENT OR LEASE | TOTAL ACRES |
|---|---|---|---|---|---|---|---|---|---|
| | SOLE OR PRIMARY | SECONDARY | SOLE OR PRIMARY | SECONDARY | | ACRES | COST ($) | | |
| **NORTH DAKOTA** | | | | | | | | | |
| APPERT LAKE | 0.00 | 0.00 | 0.00 | 0.00 | 0.00 | 0.00 | 0.00 | 907.75 | 907.75 |
| ARDOCH | 0.00 | 0.00 | 0.00 | 0.00 | 14.22 | 293.41 | 4,739.00 | 2,388.50 | 2,696.13 |
| ARROWWOOD | 4.26 | 0.00 | 11,248.72 | 0.00 | 5.34 | 2,097.51 | 46,906.56 | 2,589.01 | 15,942.86 |
| AUDUBON | 0.00 | 0.00 | 0.00 E | 14,739.19 | 0.00 | 0.00 | 0.00 | 0.00 | 14,739.19 |
| BONE HILL | 0.00 | 0.00 | 0.00 | 0.00 | 0.00 | 0.00 | 0.00 | 640.00 | 640.00 |
| BRUMBA | 0.00 | 0.00 | 0.00 | 0.00 | 0.00 | 0.00 | 0.00 | 1,977.48 | 1,977.48 |
| BUFFALO LAKE | 23.80 | 0.00 | 0.00 | 0.00 | 0.00 | 0.00 | 0.00 | 1,539.92 | 1,563.72 |
| CAMP LAKE | 0.00 | 0.00 | 0.00 | 0.00 | 0.00 | 0.00 | 0.00 | 584.70 | 584.70 |
| CANFIELD LAKE | 0.00 | 0.00 | 0.00 | 0.00 | 0.00 | 3.10 | 100.00 | 310.13 | 313.23 |
| CHASE LAKE | 0.00 | 0.00 | 0.00 | 0.00 | 0.00 | 4,449.47 | 25,611.00 | 0.00 | 4,449.47 |
| COTTONWOOD LAKE | 0.00 | 0.00 | 0.00 | 0.00 | 0.00 | 0.00 | 0.00 | 1,013.47 | 1,013.47 |
| DAKOTA LAKE | 0.00 | 0.00 | 0.00 | 0.00 | 0.00 | 0.00 | 0.00 | 2,799.78 | 2,799.78 |
| DAKOTA TALLGRASS PRAIRIE (20) | 0.00 | 0.00 | 0.00 | 0.00 | 0.00 | 0.00 | 0.00 | 4,319.94 | 4,319.94 |
| DES LACS | 100.23 | 0.00 | 13,237.02 | 0.00 | 30.00 | 701.82 | 6,893.60 | 5,478.07 | 19,547.14 |
| FLORENCE LAKE | 0.00 | 0.00 | 0.00 | 0.00 | 0.00 | 1,468.40 | 31,485.00 | 419.80 | 1,888.20 |
| FSA INTEREST ND | 0.00 | 0.00 | 0.00 | 0.00 | 0.00 | 0.00 | 0.00 | 6,906.40 | 6,906.40 |
| HALF-WAY LAKE | 0.00 | 0.00 | 0.00 | 0.00 | 0.00 | 0.00 | 0.00 | 160.00 | 160.00 |
| HIDDENWOOD | 0.00 | 0.00 | 0.00 | 0.00 | 0.00 | 0.00 | 0.00 | 568.35 | 568.35 |
| HOBART LAKE | 9.40 | 0.00 | 0.00 | 0.00 | 0.00 | 236.49 | 5,165.00 | 1,831.21 | 2,077.10 |
| HUTCHINSON LAKE | 0.00 | 0.00 | 0.00 | 0.00 | 0.00 | 0.00 | 0.00 | 478.90 | 478.90 |
| J. CLARK SALYER | 323.66 | 0.00 | 36,702.29 | 0.00 | 2.59 | 21,690.34 | 306,853.60 | 690.52 | 59,378.40 |
| JOHNSON LAKE | 0.00 | 0.00 | 0.00 | 0.00 | 4.49 | 0.00 | 0.00 | 2,003.42 | 2,007.91 |
| KELLYS SLOUGH | 680.00 | 0.00 | 0.00 | 0.00 | 0.00 | 0.00 | 0.00 | 589.50 | 1,269.50 |
| LAKE ALICE | 0.00 | 0.00 | 160.00 | 0.00 | 2.18 | 8,349.86 | 2,195,534.00 | 3,583.50 | 12,095.54 |
| LAKE GEORGE | 29.20 | 0.00 | 0.00 | 0.00 | 0.00 | 0.00 | 0.00 | 3,089.61 | 3,118.81 |
| LAKE ILO | 0.00 | 0.00 | 0.00 | 0.00 | 10.71 | 3,186.50 | 116,421.98 | 835.91 | 4,033.12 |
| LAKE NETTIE | 0.00 | 0.00 | 0.00 | 0.00 | 0.00 | 2,420.60 | 148,245.00 | 634.30 | 3,054.90 |
| LAKE OTIS | 0.00 | 0.00 | 0.00 | 0.00 | 0.00 | 0.00 | 0.00 | 320.00 | 320.00 |
| LAKE PATRICIA | 0.00 | 0.00 | 0.00 | 0.00 | 0.00 | 0.00 | 0.00 | 800.23 | 800.23 |
| LAKE ZAHL | 40.00 | 0.00 | 0.00 | 0.00 | 0.00 | 3,178.98 | 53,275.00 | 604.21 | 3,823.19 |
| LAMBS LAKE | 0.00 | 0.00 | 0.00 | 0.00 | 0.00 | 0.00 | 0.00 | 1,206.67 | 1,206.67 |
| LITTLE GOOSE | 0.00 | 0.00 | 0.00 | 0.00 | 0.00 | 0.00 | 0.00 | 288.41 | 288.41 |
| LONG LAKE | 1,170.34 | 0.00 | 0.00 | 0.00 | 0.00 | 12,736.82 | 107,180.00 | 8,589.34 | 22,496.50 |
| LORDS LAKE | 0.00 | 0.00 | 0.00 | 0.00 | 0.00 | 0.00 | 0.00 | 1,915.29 | 1,915.29 |
| LOST LAKE | 0.00 | 0.00 | 0.00 | 0.00 | 0.00 | 0.00 | 0.00 | 960.21 | 960.21 |
| LOSTWOOD | 203.60 | 0.00 | 23,395.86 | 0.00 | 0.00 | 3,304.53 | 71,553.00 | 0.00 | 26,903.99 |
| MAPLE RIVER | 0.00 | 0.00 | 0.00 | 0.00 | 0.00 | 0.00 | 0.00 | 712.00 | 712.00 |
| MCLEAN | 0.00 | 0.00 | 0.00 | 0.00 | 0.00 | 344.00 | 12,596.00 | 416.00 | 760.00 |
| NORTH DAKOTA | 0.00 | 0.00 | 0.00 | 0.00 | 0.00 | 0.00 | 0.00 | 41,660.04 | 41,660.04 |
| PLEASANT LAKE | 0.00 | 0.00 | 0.00 | 0.00 | 0.00 | 0.00 | 0.00 | 897.80 | 897.80 |
| PRETTY ROCK | 0.00 | 0.00 | 0.00 | 0.00 | 0.00 | 0.00 | 0.00 | 800.00 | 800.00 |
| RABB LAKE | 0.00 | 0.00 | 0.00 | 0.00 | 0.00 | 0.00 | 0.00 | 260.80 | 260.80 |
| ROCK LAKE | 0.00 | 0.00 | 0.00 | 0.00 | 0.00 | 0.00 | 0.00 | 5,506.96 | 5,506.96 |
| ROSE LAKE | 0.00 | 0.00 | 0.00 | 0.00 | 0.00 | 0.00 | 0.00 | 836.30 | 836.30 |
| SCHOOL SECTION LAKE | 0.00 | 0.00 | 0.00 | 0.00 | 0.00 | 0.00 | 0.00 | 297.30 | 297.30 |
| SHELL LAKE | 0.00 | 0.00 | 0.00 | 0.00 | 0.00 | 786.20 | 38,902.00 | 1,049.90 | 1,835.10 |
| SHEYENNE LAKE | 0.00 | 0.00 | 0.00 | 0.00 | 0.00 | 0.00 | 0.00 | 797.30 | 797.30 |
| SIBLEY LAKE | 0.00 | 0.00 | 0.00 | 0.00 | 0.00 | 0.00 | 0.00 | 1,077.40 | 1,077.40 |
| SILVER LAKE | 0.00 | 0.00 | 0.00 | 0.00 | 0.00 | 0.00 | 0.00 | 3,347.64 | 3,347.64 |
| SLADE | 0.00 | 0.00 | 0.00 | 0.00 | 3,000.20 | 0.00 | 0.00 | 0.00 | 3,000.20 |

TABLE 3 - NATIONAL WILDLIFE REFUGES

| STATE AND UNIT | RESERVED FROM PUBLIC DOMAIN | | ACQUIRED BY OTHER FEDERAL AGENCY | | DEVISE OR GIFT | PURCHASED | | AGREEMENT EASEMENT OR LEASE | TOTAL ACRES |
|---|---|---|---|---|---|---|---|---|---|
| | SOLE OR PRIMARY | SECONDARY | SOLE OR PRIMARY | SECONDARY | | ACRES | COST ($) | | |
| **NORTH DAKOTA** | | | | | | | | | |
| SNYDER LAKE | 0.00 | 0.00 | 0.00 | 0.00 | 0.00 | 0.00 | 0.00 | 1,550.18 | 1,550.18 |
| SPRINGWATER | 0.00 | 0.00 | 0.00 | 0.00 | 0.00 | 0.00 | 0.00 | 640.00 | 640.00 |
| STEWART LAKE | 0.00 | 0.00 | 0.00 | 0.00 | 0.00 | 636.01 | 92,270.00 | 1,590.40 | 2,226.40 |
| STONEY SLOUGH | 0.00 | 0.00 | 0.00 | 0.00 | 0.00 | 0.00 | 0.00 | 880.00 | 880.00 |
| STORM LAKE | 0.00 | 0.00 | 0.00 | 0.00 | 0.00 | 1.70 | 161.00 | 684.20 | 685.90 |
| STUMP LAKE | 27.39 | 0.00 | 0.00 | 0.00 | 0.00 | 0.00 | 0.00 | 0.00 | 27.39 |
| SULLYS HILL | 1,673.85 | 0.00 | 0.00 | 0.00 | 0.00 | 0.00 | 0.00 | 1.29 | 1,675.14 |
| SUNBURST LAKE | 0.00 | 0.00 | 0.00 | 0.00 | 0.00 | 0.00 | 0.00 | 327.51 | 327.51 |
| TEWAUKON | 1.48 | 0.00 | 0.00 | 0.00 | 20.35 | 6,836.95 | 480,122.00 | 1,505.49 | 8,363.62 |
| TOMAHAWK | 0.00 | 0.00 | 0.00 | 0.00 | 0.00 | 0.00 | 0.00 | 440.00 | 440.00 |
| UPPER SOURIS | 140.17 | 0.00 | 28,798.43 | 0.00 | 7.36 | 3,198.99 | 41,220.00 | 216.30 | 32,382.25 |
| WHITE LAKE | 0.00 | 0.00 | 0.00 | 0.00 | 0.00 | 1,040.00 | 28,800.00 | 0.00 | 1,040.00 |
| WILD RICE LAKE | 0.00 | 0.00 | 0.00 | 0.00 | 0.00 | 0.00 | 0.00 | 778.80 | 778.80 |
| WILLOW LAKE | 0.00 | 0.00 | 0.00 | 0.00 | 0.69 | 0.00 | 0.00 | 2,619.69 | 2,620.38 |
| WINTERING RIVER | 0.00 | 0.00 | 0.00 | 0.00 | 0.00 | 0.00 | 0.00 | 239.26 | 239.26 |
| WOOD LAKE | 0.00 | 0.00 | 0.00 | 0.00 | 0.00 | 0.00 | 0.00 | 280.00 | 280.00 |
| STATE TOTAL    65 | 4,444.40 | 0.00 | 113,502.32 | 14,739.19 | 3,100.12 | 76,860.03 | 3,797,863.76 | 130,496.09 | 343,145.15 |
| **OHIO** | | | | | | | | | |
| CEDAR POINT | 0.00 | 0.00 | 0.00 | 0.00 | 2,445.42 | 0.00 | 0.00 | 4.35 | 2,449.77 |
| OTTAWA | 0.00 | 0.00 | 0.00 | 0.00 | 0.00 | 5,960.39 | 4,433,893.56 | 590.85 | 6,551.24 |
| WEST SISTER ISLAND | 77.13 | 0.00 | 0.00 | 0.00 | 0.00 | 0.00 | 0.00 | 3.00 | 80.13 |
| STATE TOTAL    3 | 77.13 | 0.00 | 0.00 | 0.00 | 2,445.42 | 5,960.28 | 4,433,893.56 | 598.20 | 9,081.14 |
| **OKLAHOMA** | | | | | | | | | |
| DEEP FORK | 0.00 | 0.00 | 0.00 | 0.00 | 291.81 | 8,700.56 | 2,158,800.00 | 0.00 | 8,992.37 |
| LITTLE RIVER | 0.00 | 0.00 | 0.00 | 0.00 | 0.00 | 13,560.04 | 51,800,445.31 | 0.00 | 13,600.04 |
| OPTIMA | 0.00 | 0.00 | 0.00 E | 4,332.81 | 0.00 | 0.00 | 0.00 | 0.00 | 4,332.81 |
| OZARK PLATEAU | 0.00 | 0.00 | 256.00 | 0.00 | 420.00 | 2,556.04 | 587,195.30 | 403.53 | 3,635.57 |
| SALT PLAINS | 19,314.09 | 0.00 | 0.00 E | 11,565.28 | 30.55 | 1,117.39 | 50,837.00 | 29.81 | 32,057.12 |
| SEQUOYAH | 0.00 | 0.00 | 0.00 E | 20,800.00 | 0.00 | 0.00 | 0.00 | 0.00 | 20,800.00 |
| TISHOMINGO | 0.00 | 0.00 | 0.00 E | 16,464.18 | 0.00 | 0.00 | 0.00 | 0.00 | 16,464.18 |
| WASHITA | 0.00 | 0.00 | 0.00 R | 8,061.81 | 0.00 | 13.56 | 6,780.00 | 0.00 | 8,075.37 |
| WICHITA MOUNTAINS | 58,652.11 | 0.00 | 367.49 | 0.00 | 0.00 | 0.00 | 0.00 | 0.00 | 59,019.60 |
| STATE TOTAL    9 | 77,966.20 | 0.00 | 622.49 | 61,224.08 | 742.36 | 26,048.59 | 13,637,027.31 | 433.34 | 187,038.06 |
| **OREGON** | | | | | | | | | |
| ANKENY | 0.00 | 0.00 | 0.00 | 0.00 | 0.00 | 2,796.33 | 893,600.00 | 0.00 | 2,796.33 |
| BANDON MARSH | 0.00 | 0.00 | 0.00 | 0.00 | 34.26 | 854.70 | 1,765,028.00 | 0.00 | 888.96 |
| BASKETT SLOUGH | 0.00 | 0.00 | 0.00 | 0.00 | 0.00 | 2,492.33 | 941,585.00 | 0.00 | 2,492.33 |
| BEAR VALLEY | 0.00 | 0.00 | 0.00 | 0.00 | 0.00 | 4,198.08 | 3,298,024.00 | 2.18 | 4,200.26 |
| CAPE MEARES | 138.51 | 0.00 | 0.00 | 0.00 | 0.00 | 0.00 | 0.00 | 0.00 | 138.51 |
| COLD SPRINGS | 50.00 R | 1,748.15 | 0.00 R | 931.80 | 0.00 | 386.88 | 2,780.00 | 0.00 | 3,116.83 |
| DEER FLAT    (21) | 162.44 | 0.00 | 0.00 | 0.00 | 25.50 | 0.00 | 0.00 | 0.00 | 187.94 |
| FSA INTEREST OR | 0.00 | 0.00 | 269.00 | 0.00 | 0.00 | 0.00 | 0.00 | 338.05 | 607.05 |
| HART MOUNTAIN | 263,855.79 LM | 1,961.76 | 807.95 | 0.00 | 806.18 | 82,671.92 | 2,814,274.98 | 0.00 | 269,923.58 |
| JULIA BUTLER HANSEN    (26) | 0.00 | 0.00 | 0.00 | 0.00 | 609.03 | 2,367.74 | 2,150,550.00 | 249.61 | 3,226.38 |
| KLAMATH MARSH | 0.00 | 0.00 | 0.00 | 0.00 | 0.00 | 40,884.98 | 11,321,907.00 | 0.00 | 40,884.98 |
| LEWIS AND CLARK | 0.00 | 0.00 | 4,530.14 | 0.00 | 4,782.08 | 2,880.63 | 469,250.00 | 4.00 | 12,196.85 |
| LOWER KLAMATH    (2) | 6,618.13 | 0.00 | 0.00 | 0.00 | 0.00 | 0.00 | 0.00 | 0.00 | 6,618.13 |
| MALHEUR | 57,898.48 | 0.00 | 55,929.86 | 0.00 | 243.00 | 73,027.67 | 3,239,576.60 | 30.93 | 187,126.94 |
| MCKAY CREEK | 23.50 | 0.00 | 0.00 R | 1,813.00 | 0.00 | 0.00 | 0.00 | 0.00 | 1,836.50 |

TABLE 3 - NATIONAL WILDLIFE REFUGES

| STATE AND UNIT | RESERVED FROM PUBLIC DOMAIN | | ACQUIRED BY OTHER FEDERAL AGENCY | | DEVISE OR GIFT | PURCHASED | | AGREEMENT EASEMENT OR LEASE | TOTAL ACRES |
|---|---|---|---|---|---|---|---|---|---|
| | SOLE OR PRIMARY | SECONDARY | SOLE OR PRIMARY | SECONDARY | | ACRES | COST ($) | | |
| **OREGON** | | | | | | | | | |
| NESTUCCA BAY | 0.00 | 0.00 | 30.70 | 0.00 | 27.50 | 753.87 | 1,938,402.00 | 0.00 | 812.07 |
| OREGON ISLANDS | 925.08 | 0.00 | 0.00 | 0.00 | 0.41 | 151.82 | 4,890,000.00 | 2.32 | 1,079.61 |
| SHELDON | (15) | 0.00 | 0.00 | 0.00 | 0.00 | 0.00 | 627.48 | 4,079.00 | 0.00 | 627.48 |
| SILETZ BAY | 0.00 | 0.00 | 0.00 | 0.00 | 42.00 | 420.12 | 1,693,400.00 | 57.22 | 519.37 |
| THREE ARCH ROCKS | 15.00 | 0.00 | 0.00 | 0.00 | 0.00 | 0.00 | 0.00 | 0.00 | 15.00 |
| TUALATIN RIVER | 0.00 | 0.00 | 0.00 | 0.00 | 42.50 | 1,257.23 | 8,832,306.12 | 72.20 | 1,381.93 |
| UMATILLA | (25) | 0.00 E | 348.37 | 1,449.40 E | 7,082.00 | 0.00 | 27.60 | 33,000.00 | 0.00 | 8,907.37 |
| UPPER KLAMATH | 10,655.31 | 0.00 | 0.00 | 0.00 | 0.00 | 4,310.85 | 123,478.00 | 0.00 | 14,966.16 |
| WILLIAM L. FINLEY | 0.00 | 0.00 | 0.00 | 0.00 | 0.00 | 5,665.96 | 2,480,800.00 | 7.15 | 5,673.11 |
| STATE TOTAL 20 | 260,342.22 | 4,048.28 | 63,047.05 | 9,826.80 | 6,439.47 | 225,746.19 | 47,452,470.79 | 753.66 | 570,573.67 |
| **PENNSYLVANIA** | | | | | | | | | |
| ERIE | 0.00 | 0.00 | 0.00 | 0.00 | 0.00 | 8,800.23 | 1,612,971.64 | 0.00 | 8,800.23 |
| JOHN HEINZ | 0.00 | 0.00 | 87.26 | 0.00 | 243.14 | 662.77 | 8,146,763.80 | 0.00 | 993.17 |
| OHIO RIVER ISLANDS | (34) | 0.00 | 0.00 | 0.00 | 0.00 | 0.00 | 55.20 | 82,505.00 | 0.00 | 55.20 |
| STATE TOTAL 2 | 0.00 | 0.00 | 87.26 | 0.00 | 243.14 | 9,518.20 | 9,842,235.44 | 0.00 | 9,848.60 |
| **RHODE ISLAND** | | | | | | | | | |
| BLOCK ISLAND | 0.00 | 0.00 | 26.30 | 0.00 | 0.00 | 86.42 | 6,105,000.00 | 20.00 | 132.72 |
| JOHN H. CHAFEE | 0.00 | 0.00 | 0.00 | 0.00 | 41.39 | 394.39 | 2,243,700.00 | 0.19 | 435.97 |
| NINIGRET | 0.00 | 0.00 | 398.66 | 0.00 | 0.00 | 468.66 | 5,919,000.00 | 0.62 | 867.94 |
| SACHUEST POINT | 0.00 | 0.00 | 157.00 | 0.00 | 62.80 | 22.10 | 0.00 | 0.00 | 241.90 |
| TRUSTOM POND | 0.00 | 0.00 | 0.00 | 0.00 | 526.70 | 115.00 | 868,000.00 | 135.58 | 777.30 |
| STATE TOTAL 5 | 0.00 | 0.00 | 581.96 | 0.00 | 630.89 | 1,086.59 | 20,135,700.00 | 156.39 | 2,455.83 |
| **SOUTH CAROLINA** | | | | | | | | | |
| CAPE ROMAIN | 0.00 | 0.00 | 5,242.36 | 0.00 | 6,551.00 | 23,313.82 | 847,916.18 | 31,180.00 | 66,287.18 |
| CAROLINA SANDHILLS | 0.00 | 0.00 | 44,106.73 | 0.00 | 0.00 | 1,401.52 | 129,036.75 | 0.00 | 45,508.25 |
| ERNEST F. HOLLINGS ACE BASIN | 0.00 | 0.00 | 0.00 | 0.00 | 0.00 | 11,836.21 | 12,447,540.79 | 0.00 | 11,836.21 |
| FSA INTEREST SC | ** | 0.00 | 0.00 | 200.30 | 0.00 | 0.00 | 0.00 | 0.00 | 1,229.74 | 1,430.04 |
| PINCKNEY ISLAND | 0.00 | 0.00 | 0.00 | 0.00 | 1,324.70 | 0.00 | 0.00 | 2,728.00 | 4,052.70 |
| SANTEE | 0.00 | 0.00 | 0.00 | 0.00 | 0.00 | 4,413.28 | 568,950.57 | 8,070.00 | 12,483.28 |
| SAVANNAH | (8) | 0.00 | 0.00 | 5,604.68 | 0.00 | 37.10 | 9,345.09 | 3,667,523.54 | 24.30 | 95,011.37 |
| TYBEE | 0.00 | 0.00 | 0.00 E | 100.00 | 0.00 | 0.00 | 0.00 | 0.00 | 100.00 |
| WACCAMAW | 0.00 | 0.00 | 0.00 | 0.00 | 670.50 | 9,770.02 | 13,771,608.70 | 7,862.14 | 18,302.66 |
| STATE TOTAL 7 | 0.00 | 0.00 | 55,184.27 | 100.00 | 8,760.30 | 60,049.54 | 29,433,509.52 | 50,894.18 | 175,011.69 |
| **SOUTH DAKOTA** | | | | | | | | | |
| BEAR BUTTE | 0.00 | 0.00 | 0.00 | 0.00 | 0.00 | 0.00 | 0.00 | 374.20 | 374.20 |
| DAKOTA TALLGRASS PRAIRIE | (44) | 0.00 | 0.00 | 0.00 | 0.00 | 0.00 | 0.00 | 0.00 | 51,530.36 | 51,530.36 |
| FSA INTEREST SD | ** | 0.00 | 0.00 | 0.00 | 0.00 | 0.00 | 0.00 | 0.00 | 151.20 | 151.20 |
| KARL E. MUNDT | (90) | 0.00 | 0.00 | 0.00 | 0.00 | 738.82 | 0.00 | 0.00 | 305.00 | 1,043.82 |
| LACREEK | 0.00 | 0.00 | 6,807.47 | 0.00 | 223.11 | 9,379.75 | 788,491.00 | 445.00 | 16,855.33 |
| LAKE ANDES | 0.00 | 0.00 | 320.28 | 0.00 | 0.00 | 817.64 | 92,322.00 | 4,701.53 | 5,839.43 |
| SAND LAKE | 80.00 | 0.00 | 17,449.24 | 0.00 | 0.00 | 3,970.58 | 164,922.00 | 320.37 | 21,820.19 |
| WAUBAY | 0.00 | 0.00 | 3,966.92 | 0.00 | 0.00 | 683.77 | 23,838.00 | 90.53 | 4,740.22 |
| STATE TOTAL 8 | 80.00 | 0.00 | 28,542.89 | 0.00 | 961.93 | 14,651.74 | 1,069,573.00 | 57,918.18 | 102,154.74 |
| **TENNESSEE** | | | | | | | | | |
| CHICKASAW | 0.00 | 0.00 | 0.00 | 0.00 | 87.73 | 20,112.63 | 22,543,982.72 | 5,387.90 | 25,588.26 |
| CROSS CREEKS | 0.00 | 0.00 | 6,327.77 E | 2,442.00 | 0.00 | 91.72 | 28,290.00 | 0.00 | 8,861.49 |
| FSA INTEREST TN | ** | 0.00 | 0.00 | 112.98 | 0.00 | 0.00 | 0.00 | 0.00 | 572.41 | 685.39 |
| HATCHIE | 0.00 | 0.00 | 0.00 | 0.00 | 0.00 | 11,596.10 | 5,862,329.25 | 0.00 | 11,596.10 |
| LAKE ISOM | 0.00 | 0.00 | 1,485.12 | 0.00 | 0.00 | 360.84 | 27,290.72 | 0.00 | 1,845.96 |

TABLE 3 - NATIONAL WILDLIFE REFUGES

| STATE AND UNIT | RESERVED FROM PUBLIC DOMAIN | | ACQUIRED BY OTHER FEDERAL AGENCY | | DEVISE OR GIFT | PURCHASED | | AGREEMENT EASEMENT OR LEASE | TOTAL ACRES |
|---|---|---|---|---|---|---|---|---|---|
| | SOLE OR PRIMARY | SECONDARY | SOLE OR PRIMARY | SECONDARY | | ACRES | COST ($) | | |
| **TENNESSEE** | | | | | | | | | |
| LOWER HATCHIE | 0.00 | 0.00 | 0.00 | 0.00 | 8.26 | 9,347.06 | 13,346,016.00 | 1,872.98 | 11,828.30 |
| REELFOOT (22) | 0.00 | 0.00 | 0.00 | 0.00 | 0.00 | 563.43 | 279,531.78 | 7,847.31 | 8,450.74 |
| TENNESSEE | 0.00 | 0.00 | 0.00 T | 50,880.30 | 0.00 | 527.67 | 297,547.10 | 1.43 | 51,359.46 |
| STATE TOTAL 6 | 0.00 | 0.00 | 7,925.87 | 53,272.30 | 95.99 | 43,159.47 | 38,332,491.57 | 15,682.07 | 120,135.70 |
| **TEXAS** | | | | | | | | | |
| ANAHUAC | 0.00 | 0.00 | 0.00 | 0.00 | 362.57 | 33,923.88 | 13,983,874.47 | 43.09 | 34,329.54 |
| ARANSAS | 0.00 | 0.00 | 79,014.59 | 0.00 | 7,567.92 | 62,906.97 | 57,166,818.80 | 24,893.00 | 114,412.06 |
| ATTWATER PRAIRIE CHICKEN | 0.00 | 0.00 | 0.00 | 0.00 | 2,633.30 | 7,904.50 | 6,428,029.65 | 0.00 | 10,537.80 |
| BALCONES CANYONLANDS | 0.00 | 0.00 | 0.00 | 0.00 | 0.00 | 19,403.60 | 26,781,861.66 | 1,944.23 | 21,347.83 |
| BIG BOGGY | 0.00 | 0.00 | 0.00 | 0.00 | 0.00 | 4,216.29 | 2,457,398.19 | 309.88 | 4,526.17 |
| BRAZORIA | 0.00 | 0.00 | 0.00 | 0.00 | 25.00 | 44,220.20 | 14,864,988.26 | 168.58 | 44,413.88 |
| BUFFALO LAKE | 0.00 | 0.00 | 7,663.93 | 0.00 | 0.00 | 0.00 | 0.00 | 0.23 | 7,664.16 |
| CADDO LAKE | 0.00 | 0.00 | 6,262.24 A | 2,211.76 | 0.00 | 0.00 | 0.00 | 0.00 | 8,414.00 |
| FSA INTEREST TX ** | 0.00 | 0.00 | 1,878.13 | 0.00 | 0.00 | 0.00 | 0.00 | 0.00 | 1,878.13 |
| GRULLA (17) | 0.00 | 0.00 | 0.00 | 0.00 | 0.00 | 4.97 | 5,000.00 | 0.00 | 4.97 |
| HAGERMAN | 0.00 | 0.00 | 0.00 E | 11,319.84 | 0.00 | 0.00 | 0.00 | 0.00 | 11,319.84 |
| LAGUNA ATASCOSA | 0.00 | 0.00 | 8,486.00 | 0.00 | 0.00 | 78,241.17 | 53,544,315.84 | 113.13 | 86,840.27 |
| LITTLE SANDY | 0.00 | 0.00 | 0.00 | 0.00 | 0.00 | 0.00 | 0.00 | 3,802.00 | 3,802.00 |
| LOWER RIO GRANDE VALLEY | 0.00 | 0.00 | 46.18 | 0.00 | 1,640.41 | 76,688.54 | 70,548,797.50 | 10,979.81 | 89,354.54 |
| MCFADDIN | 0.00 | 0.00 | 0.00 | 0.00 | 0.00 | 51,112.55 | 10,966,489.20 | 7,748.88 | 58,861.43 |
| MOODY | 0.00 | 0.00 | 0.00 | 0.00 | 0.00 | 0.00 | 0.00 | 3,516.67 | 3,516.87 |
| MULESHOE | 0.00 | 0.00 | 3,654.30 | 0.00 | 0.00 | 2,154.80 | 25,740.00 | 0.00 | 5,809.10 |
| NECHES RIVER | 0.00 | 0.00 | 0.00 | 0.00 | 0.00 | 0.00 | 0.00 | 1.00 | 1.00 |
| SAN BERNARD | 0.00 | 0.00 | 0.00 | 0.00 | 2,142.87 | 39,347.05 | 18,670,108.19 | 442.12 | 41,732.04 |
| SANTA ANA | 0.00 | 0.00 | 0.00 | 0.00 | 37.06 | 2,049.91 | 201,516.00 | 0.53 | 2,087.50 |
| TEXAS POINT | 0.00 | 0.00 | 0.00 | 0.00 | 0.00 | 8,952.02 | 1,719,000.00 | 0.00 | 8,952.02 |
| TRINITY RIVER | 0.00 | 0.00 | 0.00 | 0.00 | 0.00 | 20,861.86 | 13,303,253.00 | 0.00 | 20,861.86 |
| STATE TOTAL 20 | 0.00 | 0.00 | 46,044.97 | 13,531.60 | 14,399.13 | 451,817.91 | 209,039,188.76 | 53,983.42 | 580,677.03 |
| **UTAH** | | | | | | | | | |
| BEAR RIVER | 43,442.89 | 0.00 | 0.00 | 0.00 | 4,285.43 | 26,023.86 | 4,002,163.47 | 46.54 | 73,798.82 |
| COLORADO RIVER (46) | 0.00 | 0.00 | 0.00 | 0.00 | 0.00 | 0.00 | 0.00 | 1,008.10 | 1,008.10 |
| FISH SPRINGS | 14,217.42 | 0.00 | 0.00 | 0.00 | 0.00 | 3,774.82 | 93,325.00 | 0.00 | 17,992.24 |
| FSA INTEREST UT ** | 0.00 | 0.00 | 0.00 | 0.00 | 0.00 | 0.00 | 0.00 | 280.84 | 280.84 |
| OURAY | 3,111.68 | 0.00 | 161.68 | 0.00 | 0.00 | 5,014.98 | 467,084.25 | 3,850.50 | 12,138.24 |
| STATE TOTAL 4 | 60,771.30 | 0.00 | 161.68 | 0.00 | 4,285.43 | 34,813.66 | 4,562,572.72 | 5,186.08 | 105,298.24 |
| **VERMONT** | | | | | | | | | |
| FSA INTEREST VT ** | 0.00 | 0.00 | 0.00 | 0.00 | 0.00 | 0.00 | 0.00 | 71.00 | 71.00 |
| MISSISQUOI | 0.00 | 0.00 | 0.00 | 0.00 | 264.50 | 6,306.08 | 341,134.27 | 0.00 | 6,570.58 |
| SILVIO O. CONTE (45) | 0.00 | 0.00 | 0.00 | 0.00 | 81.86 | 26,492.25 | 7,009,583.10 | 0.00 | 26,574.11 |
| STATE TOTAL 2 | 0.00 | 0.00 | 0.00 | 0.00 | 346.36 | 32,798.33 | 7,350,717.37 | 71.00 | 33,215.69 |
| **VIRGINIA** | | | | | | | | | |
| BACK BAY | 0.00 | 0.00 | 0.00 | 0.00 | 2.36 | 9,032.65 | 23,463,814.08 | 0.00 | 9,035.01 |
| CHINCOTEAGUE (23) | 0.00 | 0.00 | 0.23 | 0.00 | 1,434.85 | 11,579.60 | 8,316,070.18 | 600.00 | 13,614.68 |
| EASTERN SHORE OF VIRGINIA | 0.00 | 0.00 | 175.33 | 0.00 | 70.35 | 902.32 | 6,132,443.00 | 5.27 | 1,153.27 |
| FEATHERSTONE | 0.00 | 0.00 | 0.00 | 0.00 | 161.92 | 163.90 | 486,800.00 | 0.00 | 325.82 |
| FISHERMAN ISLAND | 0.00 | 0.00 | 1,025.00 | 0.00 | 0.00 | 871.30 | 1,600,000.00 | 0.00 | 1,896.30 |
| FSA INTEREST VA ** | 0.00 | 0.00 | 0.00 | 0.00 | 0.00 | 0.00 | 0.00 | 133.70 | 133.70 |
| GREAT DISMAL SWAMP (24) | 0.00 | 0.00 | 27.14 | 0.00 | 49,097.01 | 35,968.96 | 17,198,270.15 | 0.00 | 85,093.11 |
| JAMES RIVER | 0.00 | 0.00 | 0.00 | 0.00 | 0.00 | 4,199.58 | 5,966,072.00 | 0.00 | 4,199.58 |

TABLE 3 - NATIONAL WILDLIFE REFUGES

| STATE AND UNIT | | RESERVED FROM PUBLIC DOMAIN | | ACQUIRED BY OTHER FEDERAL AGENCY | | DEVISE OR GIFT | PURCHASED | | AGREEMENT EASEMENT OR LEASE | TOTAL ACRES |
|---|---|---|---|---|---|---|---|---|---|---|
| | | SOLE OR PRIMARY | SECONDARY | SOLE OR PRIMARY | SECONDARY | | ACRES | COST ($) | | |
| **VIRGINIA** | | | | | | | | | | |
| MACKAY ISLAND | (26) | 0.00 | 0.00 | 0.00 | 0.00 | 0.00 | 874.40 | 26,856.75 | 0.00 | 874.40 |
| MARTIN | (23) | 0.00 | 0.00 | 0.00 | 0.00 | 545.62 | 0.00 | 0.00 | 0.00 | 545.62 |
| MASON NECK | | 0.00 | 0.00 | 0.00 | 0.00 | 0.00 | 1,487.72 | 7,235,368.50 | 789.06 | 2,276.78 |
| NANSEMOND | | 0.00 | 0.00 | 422.99 | 0.00 | 0.00 | 0.00 | 11,350.00 | 0.00 | 422.99 |
| OCCOQUAN BAY | | 0.00 | 0.00 | 642.07 | 0.00 | 0.00 | 0.00 | 0.00 | 0.00 | 642.07 |
| PLUM TREE ISLAND | | 0.00 | 0.00 | 3,275.60 | 0.00 | 15.08 | 211.00 | 105,900.00 | 0.00 | 3,501.68 |
| PRESQUILE | | 0.00 | 0.00 | 0.00 | 0.00 | 1,328.92 | 0.00 | 0.00 | 0.00 | 1,328.92 |
| RAPPAHANNOCK RIVER VALLEY | | 0.00 | 0.00 | 0.00 | 0.00 | 1,336.84 | 4,981.12 | 10,210,608.11 | 1,403.52 | 7,721.48 |
| WALLOPS ISLAND | | 0.00 | 0.00 | 373.00 | 0.00 | 0.00 | 0.00 | 0.00 | 3,000.00 | 3,373.00 |
| STATE TOTAL | 13 | 0.00 | 0.00 | 5,941.36 | 0.00 | 53,594.95 | 70,272.55 | 81,753,372.75 | 5,931.55 | 135,740.41 |
| **WASHINGTON** | | | | | | | | | | |
| COLUMBIA | | 10,978.11 R | 5,287.11 | 0.00 R | 1,274.59 | 0.00 | 15,062.00 | 458,001.04 | 804.37 | 29,506.27 |
| CONBOY LAKE | | 0.00 | 0.00 | 0.00 | 0.00 | 80.00 | 6,271.41 | 2,864,410.00 | 718.29 | 7,069.70 |
| COPALIS | | 60.80 | 0.00 | 0.00 | 0.00 | 0.00 | 0.00 | 0.00 | 0.00 | 60.80 |
| DUNGENESS | | 202.50 CO | 32.50 | 0.00 | 0.00 | 128.66 | 84.22 | 756,500.00 | 324.64 | 772.52 |
| FLATTERY ROCKS | | 125.00 | 0.00 | 0.00 | 0.00 | 0.00 | 0.00 | 0.00 | 0.00 | 125.00 |
| FRANZ LAKE | | 0.00 | 0.00 | 0.00 | 0.00 | 0.00 | 550.33 | 1,143,700.00 | 1.40 | 551.73 |
| FSA INTEREST WA | ** | 0.00 | 0.00 | 466.43 | 0.00 | 0.00 | 0.00 | 0.00 | 499.49 | 965.92 |
| GRAYS HARBOR | | 0.00 | 0.00 | 0.00 | 0.00 | 0.00 | 1,407.77 | 1,039,800.00 | 63.61 | 1,471.38 |
| JULIA BUTLER HANSEN | (4) | 0.00 | 0.00 | 0.00 | 0.00 | 0.00 | 2,888.78 | 1,980,321.00 | 155.56 | 3,044.44 |
| LITTLE PEND OREILLE | | 8,790.40 | 0.00 | 27,369.33 | 0.00 | 0.00 | 6,443.84 | 626,425.00 | 0.00 | 42,593.57 |
| MCNARY | | 0.00 | 0.00 | 3,108.71 E | 11,856.00 | 5.49 | 468.19 | 1,032,435.00 | 30.00 | 15,505.39 |
| NISQUALLY | | 0.00 | 0.00 | 486.25 | 0.00 | 121.19 | 3,630.33 | 10,228,826.32 | 32.36 | 4,270.13 |
| PIERCE | | 0.00 | 0.00 | 0.00 | 0.00 | 319.00 | 10.38 | 525,000.00 | 0.00 | 329.38 |
| PROTECTION ISLAND | | 0.00 | 0.00 | 0.00 | 0.00 | 1.42 | 317.89 | 3,624,066.00 | 340.00 | 659.31 |
| QUILLAYUTE NEEDLES | | 300.20 | 0.00 | 0.00 | 0.00 | 0.00 | 0.00 | 0.00 | 0.00 | 300.20 |
| RIDGEFIELD | | 0.00 | 0.00 | 0.00 | 0.00 | 24.99 | 5,190.97 | 5,314,600.00 | 1.74 | 5,217.70 |
| SADDLE MOUNTAIN | | 0.00 DOE | 470.00 | 0.00 DOE | 161,045.93 | 0.00 | 0.00 | 0.00 | 0.00 | 161,485.93 |
| SAN JUAN ISLANDS | | 448.53 | 0.00 | 0.00 | 0.00 | 0.00 | 0.00 | 0.00 | 0.00 | 448.53 |
| STEIGERWALD LAKE | | 0.00 | 0.00 | 632.44 | 0.00 | 0.00 | 413.58 | 2,793,000.00 | 0.00 | 1,046.02 |
| TOPPENISH | | 0.00 | 0.00 | 0.00 | 0.00 | 0.00 | 1,977.55 | 715,137.00 | 1.29 | 1,978.84 |
| TURNBULL | | 0.00 | 0.00 | 0.00 | 0.00 | 0.00 | 15,858.92 | 1,296,880.48 | 2,025.78 | 17,804.70 |
| UMATILLA | (4) | 0.00 E | 102.50 | 1,466.83 E | 13,107.00 | 0.00 | 0.00 | 0.00 | 200.50 | 14,875.83 |
| WILLAPA | | 2,058.90 | 0.00 | 0.00 | 0.00 | 892.00 | 10,364.72 | 7,344,607.34 | 3,122.81 | 19,435.43 |
| STATE TOTAL | 20 | 22,964.44 | 1,992.11 | 33,016.99 | 187,322.82 | 1,572.75 | 70,937.87 | 41,215,858.58 | 8,461.64 | 326,738.72 |
| **WEST VIRGINIA** | | | | | | | | | | |
| CANAAN VALLEY | | 0.00 | 0.00 | 0.00 | 0.00 | 6.60 | 15,875.67 | 33,186,153.00 | 18.97 | 15,901.24 |
| FSA INTEREST WV | ** | 0.00 | 0.00 | 0.00 | 0.00 | 0.00 | 0.00 | 0.00 | 8.37 | 8.37 |
| OHIO RIVER ISLANDS | (36) | 0.00 | 0.00 | 18.90 | 0.00 | 307.37 | 2,270.20 | 4,079,242.10 | 1.00 | 2,597.47 |
| STATE TOTAL | 2 | 0.00 | 0.00 | 18.90 | 0.00 | 313.97 | 18,145.87 | 37,265,395.10 | 28.34 | 18,507.08 |
| **WISCONSIN** | | | | | | | | | | |
| FOX RIVER | | 0.00 | 0.00 | 0.00 | 0.00 | 0.00 | 874.48 | 654,333.00 | 0.00 | 874.48 |
| FSA INTEREST WI | ** | 0.00 | 0.00 | 900.00 | 0.00 | 0.00 | 0.00 | 0.00 | 0.00 | 900.00 |
| GRAVEL ISLAND | | 27.00 | 0.00 | 0.00 | 0.00 | 0.00 | 0.00 | 0.00 | 0.00 | 27.00 |
| GREEN BAY | | 2.00 | 0.00 | 0.00 | 0.00 | 0.00 | 0.00 | 0.00 | 0.00 | 2.00 |
| HORICON | | 0.00 | 0.00 | 0.00 | 0.00 | 9.44 | 21,374.69 | 841,988.34 | 31.83 | 21,413.96 |
| NECEDAH | | 30.16 | 0.00 | 43,283.42 | 0.00 | 0.00 | 382.28 | 23,194.26 | 0.00 | 43,695.86 |
| TREMPEALEAU | | 0.00 | 0.00 | 0.00 | 0.00 | 0.00 | 6,198.83 | 905,392.50 | 0.00 | 6,198.83 |
| UPPER MISSISSIPPI RIVER | (25) | 655.57 | 0.00 | 4.23 E | 40,341.00 | 119.18 | 48,488.76 | 1,135,606.27 | 2.50 | 89,611.24 |

TABLE 3 - NATIONAL WILDLIFE REFUGES

| STATE AND UNIT | | RESERVED FROM PUBLIC DOMAIN | | ACQUIRED BY OTHER FEDERAL AGENCY | | DEVISE OR GIFT | PURCHASED | | AGREEMENT EASEMENT OR LEASE | TOTAL ACRES |
|---|---|---|---|---|---|---|---|---|---|---|
| | | SOLE OR PRIMARY | SECONDARY | SOLE OR PRIMARY | SECONDARY | | ACRES | COST ($) | | |
| **WISCONSIN** | | | | | | | | | | |
| WHITTLESEY CREEK | | 0.00 | 0.00 | 0.00 | 0.00 | 50.00 | 165.04 | 649,000.00 | 0.00 | 215.06 |
| STATE TOTAL | 7 | 714.75 | 0.00 | 44,257.65 | 43,341.00 | 174.64 | 77,564.06 | 4,236,514.30 | 36.33 | 163,058.43 |
| **WYOMING** | | | | | | | | | | |
| BAMFORTH | | 201.23 | 0.00 | 0.00 | 0.00 | 0.00 | 964.80 | 6,368.00 | 0.00 | 1,166.03 |
| COKEVILLE MEADOWS | | 0.00 | 0.00 | 0.00 | 0.00 | 0.00 | 6,465.82 | 3,105,412.76 | 2,793.50 | 9,259.32 |
| FSA INTEREST WY | ** | 0.00 | 0.00 | 0.00 | 0.00 | 0.00 | 0.00 | 0.00 | 3,287.75 | 3,287.75 |
| HUTTON LAKE | | 152.85 | 0.00 | 0.00 | 0.00 | 0.00 | 1,815.49 | 7,944.00 | 0.00 | 1,968.34 |
| MORTENSON LAKE | | 0.00 | 0.00 | 0.00 | 0.00 | 0.00 | 1,927.34 | 571,000.00 | 0.00 | 1,927.34 |
| NATIONAL ELK | | 4,676.53 | 0.00 | 0.00 | 0.00 | 4,516.60 | 15,584.17 | 7,882,177.00 | 1.01 | 24,778.31 |
| PATHFINDER | | 2,294.84 R | 11,501.57 | 0.00 R | 3,010.49 | 0.00 | 0.00 | 0.00 | 0.00 | 16,806.90 |
| SEEDSKADEE | | 10,124.29 | 0.00 | 16,078.93 | 0.00 | 0.00 | 0.00 | 0.00 | 1,026.00 | 27,230.22 |
| STATE TOTAL | 7 | 17,449.74 | 11,501.57 | 16,078.93 | 3,010.49 | 4,516.60 | 26,757.62 | 11,572,901.76 | 7,108.26 | 86,424.21 |
| **AMERICAN SAMOA** | | | | | | | | | | |
| ROSE ATOLL | | 0.00 C | 37,453.00 | 1,613.00 | 0.00 | 0.00 | 0.00 | 0.00 | 0.00 | 39,066.00 |
| STATE TOTAL | 1 | 0.00 | 37,453.00 | 1,613.00 | 0.00 | 0.00 | 0.00 | 0.00 | 0.00 | 39,066.00 |
| **GUAM** | | | | | | | | | | |
| GUAM | | 0.00 | 0.00 | 772.10 | 0.00 | 0.00 | 0.00 | 0.00 | 22,456.00 | 23,228.10 |
| STATE TOTAL | 1 | 0.00 | 0.00 | 772.10 | 0.00 | 0.00 | 0.00 | 0.00 | 22,456.00 | 23,228.10 |
| **U.S. MINOR OUTLYING ISLANDS** | | | | | | | | | | |
| BAKER ISLAND | | 0.00 | 0.00 | 31,736.89 | 0.00 | 0.00 | 0.00 | 0.00 | 0.00 | 31,736.89 |
| HOWLAND ISLAND | | 0.00 | 0.00 | 32,550.25 | 0.00 | 0.00 | 0.00 | 0.00 | 0.00 | 32,550.25 |
| JARVIS ISLAND | | 0.00 | 0.00 | 37,519.17 | 0.00 | 0.00 | 0.00 | 0.00 | 0.00 | 37,519.17 |
| JOHNSTON ISLAND | | 0.00 | 0.00 | 100.00 | 0.00 | 0.00 | 0.00 | 0.00 | 0.00 | 100.00 |
| KINGMAN REEF | | 0.00 | 0.00 | 426,392.00 | 0.00 | 0.00 | 0.00 | 0.00 | 0.00 | 426,392.00 |
| MIDWAY ATOLL | | 0.00 | 0.00 | 298,156.50 I | 262,835.00 | 0.00 | 0.00 | 0.00 | 0.00 | 580,991.50 |
| NAVASSA ISLAND | | 0.00 | 0.00 | 364,950.00 | 0.00 | 0.00 | 0.00 | 0.00 | 0.00 | 364,950.00 |
| PALMYRA ATOLL | | 0.00 | 0.00 | 503,963.00 | 0.00 | 0.00 | 443.95 | 9,500,000.00 | 2.30 | 504,409.25 |
| STATE TOTAL | 8 | 0.00 | 0.00 | 1,695,367.81 | 262,835.00 | 0.00 | 443.95 | 9,500,000.00 | 2.30 | 1,978,649.06 |
| **PUERTO RICO** | | | | | | | | | | |
| CABO ROJO | | 0.00 | 0.00 | 567.33 | 0.00 | 0.00 | 1,289.38 | 2,999,265.63 | 0.00 | 1,856.71 |
| CULEBRA | | 0.00 | 0.00 | 1,547.17 | 0.00 | 0.00 | 0.00 | 0.00 | 14.21 | 1,561.38 |
| DESECHEO | | 0.00 | 0.00 | 360.00 | 0.00 | 0.00 | 0.00 | 0.00 | 0.00 | 360.00 |
| LAGUNA CARTAGENA | | 0.00 | 0.00 | 262.86 | 0.00 | 0.00 | 0.00 | 0.00 | 772.89 | 1,035.75 |
| VIEQUES | | 0.00 | 0.00 | 17,770.62 | 0.00 | 0.00 | 0.00 | 0.00 | 0.00 | 17,770.62 |
| STATE TOTAL | 5 | 0.00 | 0.00 | 20,527.98 | 0.00 | 0.00 | 1,289.38 | 2,999,265.63 | 787.10 | 22,584.46 |
| **VIRGIN ISLANDS** | | | | | | | | | | |
| BUCK ISLAND | | 0.00 | 0.00 | 46.07 | 0.00 | 0.00 | 0.00 | 0.00 | 0.00 | 46.07 |
| GREEN CAY | | 0.00 | 0.00 | 0.00 | 0.00 | 0.00 | 13.77 | 250,000.00 | 0.00 | 13.77 |
| SANDY POINT | | 0.00 | 0.00 | 0.00 | 0.00 | 0.00 | 530.31 | 3,534,370.00 | 0.00 | 530.31 |
| STATE TOTAL | 3 | 0.00 | 0.00 | 46.07 | 0.00 | 0.00 | 544.08 | 3,784,370.00 | 0.00 | 590.15 |
| GRAND TOTAL | 547 | 81,325,231.35 | 635,408.29 | 3,160,469.36 | 1,210,809.23 | 751,913.75 | 4,272,396.08 | 1,920,573,475.17 | 1,452,495.20 | 92,808,715.26 |

TABLE 3 - NATIONAL WILDLIFE REFUGES

FOOTNOTES FOR TABLE 3

(1)  ALSO IN GEORGIA
(2)  ALSO IN CALIFORNIA
(3)  ALSO IN ARIZONA
(4)  ALSO IN OREGON
(5)  ALSO IN ALABAMA
(6)  ALSO IN FLORIDA
(7)  ALSO IN SOUTH CAROLINA
(8)  ALSO IN MISSOURI
(9)  ALSO IN IOWA, MINNESOTA AND WISCONSIN
(10) ALSO IN NEBRASKA
(11) ALSO IN ILLINOIS
(12) ALSO IN TEXAS
(13) ALSO IN ILLINOIS, MINNESOTA AND WISCONSIN
(14) ALSO IN TENNESSEE
(15) ALSO IN NEVADA
(16) ALSO IN VIRGINIA
(17) ALSO IN NEW MEXICO
(18) ALSO IN ILLINOIS, IOWA AND WISCONSIN
(19) ALSO IN IOWA
(20) ALSO IN SOUTH DAKOTA
(21) ALSO IN IDAHO
(22) ALSO IN KENTUCKY
(23) ALSO IN MARYLAND
(24) ALSO IN NORTH CAROLINA
(25) ALSO IN ILLINOIS, IOWA AND MINNESOTA
(26) ALSO IN WASHINGTON
(27) ALSO IN MISSISSIPPI
(28) ALSO IN LOUISIANA
(33) ALSO IN ILLINOIS AND IOWA
(34) ALSO IN WEST VIRGINIA AND KENTUCKY
(35) ALSO IN PENNSYLVANIA AND KENTUCKY
(37) ALSO IN NEW HAMPSHIRE
(37) ALSO IN MAINE
(38) ALSO IN WEST VIRGINIA AND PENNSYLVANIA
(39) ALSO IN NEW YORK
(40) ALSO IN NEW JERSEY
(41) ALSO IN MASSACHUSETTS AND NEW HAMPSHIRE
(42) ALSO IN VERMONT AND NEW HAMPSHIRE
(43) ALSO IN VERMONT AND MASSACHUSETTS
(44) ALSO IN NORTH DAKOTA
(45) ALSO IN UTAH
(46) ALSO IN COLORADO
(47) ALSO IN MINNESOTA

A    - DEPARTMENT OF THE ARMY
BIA  - BUREAU OF INDIAN AFFAIRS, DEPARTMENT OF THE INTERIOR
C    - DEPARTMENT OF COMMERCE
CG   - COAST GUARD, DEPARTMENT OF HOMELAND SECURITY
DOE  - DEPARTMENT OF ENERGY (FUNCTIONS FORMERLY UNDER NUCLEAR REGULATORY COMMISSION)
E    - CORPS OF ENGINEERS, DEPARTMENT OF THE ARMY
F    - FOREST SERVICE, DEPARTMENT OF AGRICULTURE
FA   - FEDERAL AVIATION ADMINISTRATION, DEPARTMENT OF TRANSPORTATION
FSA  - FARM SERVICE AGENCY (FORMERLY FARMERS HOME ADMINISTRATION, DEPARTMENT OF AGRICULTURE)
GS   - GEOLOGICAL SURVEY, DEPARTMENT OF THE INTERIOR
I    - OFFICE OF INSULAR AFFAIRS, DEPARTMENT OF THE INTERIOR
LM   - BUREAU OF LAND MANAGEMENT, DEPARTMENT OF THE INTERIOR
N    - DEPARTMENT OF THE NAVY
NA   - NATIONAL AERONAUTICS AND SPACE ADMINISTRATION
R    - BUREAU OF RECLAMATION, DEPARTMENT OF THE INTERIOR
T    - TENNESSEE VALLEY AUTHORITY

(#)* - COUNTED IN ANOTHER STATE
" "  - SUMMARY BY STATE OF ALL OTHER ACRES, BOTH FEE AND LESS THAN FEE, ACQUIRED FROM THE FSA, NOT REPORTED WITHIN AN EXISTING PROJECT.
       SUMMARY MAY CONTAIN ONE OR MORE OWNERSHIPS. FSA INTEREST STATE SUMMARY ACRES ARE INCLUDED IN THE TOTAL ACRES FOR EACH STATE
       BUT ARE NOT COUNTED AS SEPARATE UNITS IN THE NATIONAL WILDLIFE REFUGE STATE TOTALS.

TABLE 4 - WATERFOWL PRODUCTION AREAS

| STATE AND UNIT | | RESERVED FROM PUBLIC DOMAIN | | ACQUIRED BY OTHER FEDERAL AGENCY | | DEVISE OR GIFT | PURCHASED | | AGREEMENT EASEMENT OR LEASE | TOTAL ACRES |
|---|---|---|---|---|---|---|---|---|---|---|
| | | SOLE OR PRIMARY | SECONDARY | SOLE OR PRIMARY | SECONDARY | | ACRES | COST ($) | | |
| **IDAHO** | | | | | | | | | | |
| OXFORD SLOUGH | | 0.00 | 0.00 | 0.00 | 0.00 | 0.00 | 1,878.41 | 530,000.00 | 0.00 | 1,878.41 |
| WMD TOTAL | 1 | 0.00 | 0.00 | 0.00 | 0.00 | 0.00 | 1,878.41 | 530,000.00 | 0.00 | 1,878.41 |
| STATE TOTAL | 1 | 0.00 | 0.00 | 0.00 | 0.00 | 0.00 | 1,878.41 | 530,000.00 | 0.00 | 1,878.41 |
| **IOWA** | | | | | | | | | | |
| IOWA WMD | | | | | | | | | | |
| BOONE | | 0.00 | 0.00 | 0.00 | 0.00 | 0.00 | 391.33 | 566,600.00 | 0.00 | 391.33 |
| BUENA VISTA | | 0.00 | 0.00 | 0.00 | 0.00 | 0.00 | 69.09 | 169,000.00 | 0.00 | 69.09 |
| CERRO GORDO | | 0.00 | 0.00 | 0.00 | 0.00 | 0.00 | 2,720.25 | 3,294,877.82 | 5.70 | 2,725.95 |
| CLAY | | 0.00 | 0.00 | 0.00 | 0.00 | 0.00 | 867.93 | 1,146,206.85 | 0.00 | 867.93 |
| DICKINSON | | 0.00 | 0.00 | 0.00 | 0.00 | 0.65 | 5,501.10 | 7,257,777.00 | 98.00 | 5,599.75 |
| EMMET | | 0.00 | 0.00 | 0.00 | 0.00 | 0.00 | 1,811.84 | 2,483,575.00 | 58.00 | 1,869.84 |
| GREENE | | 0.00 | 0.00 | 0.00 | 0.00 | 0.00 | 669.05 | 1,280,700.00 | 0.00 | 669.05 |
| GUTHRIE | | 0.00 | 0.00 | 0.00 | 0.00 | 0.00 | 302.53 | 609,740.00 | 0.00 | 302.53 |
| HANCOCK | | 0.00 | 0.00 | 0.00 | 0.00 | 0.00 | 802.70 | 545,480.28 | 7.00 | 809.70 |
| KOSSUTH | | 0.00 | 0.00 | 0.00 | 0.00 | 0.00 | 3,114.86 | 6,613,646.98 | 23.00 | 3,137.86 |
| OSCEOLA | | 0.00 | 0.00 | 0.00 | 0.00 | 0.00 | 0.00 | 0.00 | 41.00 | 41.00 |
| PALO ALTO | | 0.00 | 0.00 | 0.00 | 0.00 | 0.00 | 674.36 | 961,082.65 | 282.00 | 956.36 |
| POCAHONTAS | | 0.00 | 0.00 | 0.00 | 0.00 | 0.00 | 654.16 | 1,716,400.00 | 0.00 | 654.16 |
| POLK | | 0.00 | 0.00 | 0.00 | 0.00 | 0.00 | 110.00 | 241,500.00 | 0.00 | 110.00 |
| SAC | | 0.00 | 0.00 | 0.00 | 0.00 | 0.00 | 629.42 | 1,209,580.00 | 0.00 | 629.42 |
| WINNEBAGO | | 0.00 | 0.00 | 0.00 | 0.00 | 0.00 | 1,023.15 | 1,138,300.31 | 105.00 | 1,128.15 |
| WORTH | | 0.00 | 0.00 | 0.00 | 0.00 | 0.00 | 1,491.84 | 1,088,329.87 | 18.00 | 1,509.84 |
| WRIGHT | | 0.00 | 0.00 | 0.00 | 0.00 | 0.00 | 1,696.65 | 2,615,725.00 | 0.00 | 1,696.65 |
| WMD TOTAL | 18 | 0.00 | 0.00 | 0.00 | 0.00 | 0.65 | 22,530.26 | 32,941,331.74 | 637.70 | 23,168.61 |
| STATE TOTAL | 18 | 0.00 | 0.00 | 0.00 | 0.00 | 0.65 | 22,530.26 | 32,941,331.74 | 637.70 | 23,168.61 |
| **MAINE** | | | | | | | | | | |
| CARLTON POND | | 0.00 | 0.00 | 0.00 | 0.00 | 0.00 | 1,068.21 | 18,276.08 | 0.00 | 1,068.21 |
| WMD TOTAL | 1 | 0.00 | 0.00 | 0.00 | 0.00 | 0.00 | 1,068.21 | 18,276.08 | 0.00 | 1,068.21 |
| STATE TOTAL | 1 | 0.00 | 0.00 | 0.00 | 0.00 | 0.00 | 1,068.21 | 18,276.08 | 0.00 | 1,068.21 |
| **MICHIGAN** | | | | | | | | | | |
| MICHIGAN WMD | | | | | | | | | | |
| JACKSON | | 0.00 | 0.00 | 0.00 | 0.00 | 138.41 | 160.00 | 170,000.00 | 0.00 | 298.41 |
| VAN BUREN | | 0.00 | 0.00 | 0.00 | 0.00 | 0.00 | 77.08 | 43,600.00 | 0.00 | 77.08 |
| WMD TOTAL | 2 | 0.00 | 0.00 | 0.00 | 0.00 | 138.41 | 237.08 | 213,600.00 | 0.00 | 375.49 |
| STATE TOTAL | 2 | 0.00 | 0.00 | 0.00 | 0.00 | 138.41 | 237.08 | 213,600.00 | 0.00 | 375.49 |
| **MINNESOTA** | | | | | | | | | | |
| BIG STONE WMD | | | | | | | | | | |
| LINCOLN | | 0.00 | 0.00 | 0.00 | 0.00 | 0.00 | 1,014.01 | 747,200.00 | 1,080.82 | 2,094.83 |
| LYON | | 0.00 | 0.00 | 0.00 | 0.00 | 0.00 | 1,553.56 | 1,260,720.00 | 335.80 | 1,889.36 |
| WMD TOTAL | 2 | 0.00 | 0.00 | 0.00 | 0.00 | 0.00 | 2,567.57 | 2,016,920.00 | 1,416.62 | 3,984.19 |
| DETROIT LAKES WMD | | | | | | | | | | |
| BECKER | | 0.00 | 0.00 | 0.00 | 0.00 | 4.33 | 12,903.70 | 4,517,570.56 | 2,531.33 | 15,439.36 |
| CLAY | | 0.00 | 0.00 | 0.00 | 0.00 | 11.17 | 10,541.45 | 3,096,045.18 | 3,477.27 | 14,029.89 |
| MAHNOMEN | | 0.00 | 0.00 | 0.00 | 0.00 | 0.00 | 6,087.33 | 1,183,558.90 | 4,784.73 | 10,872.06 |

TABLE 4 - WATERFOWL PRODUCTION AREAS

| STATE AND UNIT | RESERVED FROM PUBLIC DOMAIN | | ACQUIRED BY OTHER FEDERAL AGENCY | | DEVISE OR GIFT | PURCHASED | | AGREEMENT EASEMENT OR LEASE | TOTAL ACRES |
| | SOLE OR PRIMARY | SECONDARY | SOLE OR PRIMARY | SECONDARY | | ACRES | COST ($) | | |
|---|---|---|---|---|---|---|---|---|---|
| **MINNESOTA** | | | | | | | | | |
| DETROIT LAKES WMD | | | | | | | | | |
| NORMAN | 0.00 | 0.00 | 0.00 | 0.00 | 0.00 | 1,120.00 | 400,000.00 | 0.00 | 1,120.00 |
| POLK | 0.00 | 0.00 | 0.00 | 0.00 | 0.00 | 12,972.81 | 2,872,752.86 | 1,819.80 | 14,792.61 |
| WMD TOTAL 5 | 0.00 | 0.00 | 0.00 | 0.00 | 15.50 | 43,625.29 | 12,068,927.50 | 12,613.13 | 56,253.92 |
| FERGUS FALLS WMD | | | | | | | | | |
| DOUGLAS | 0.00 | 0.00 | 0.00 | 0.00 | 0.00 | 9,955.97 | 2,740,245.20 | 6,197.41 | 16,153.38 |
| GRANT | 0.00 | 0.00 | 0.00 | 0.00 | 0.00 | 10,217.87 | 2,969,508.12 | 3,651.26 | 13,869.13 |
| OTTER TAIL | 0.00 | 0.00 | 0.00 | 0.00 | 52.19 | 20,915.28 | 6,968,572.26 | 14,728.75 | 35,696.22 |
| WILKIN | 0.00 | 0.00 | 0.00 | 0.00 | 0.00 | 2,433.26 | 900,064.35 | 309.00 | 2,742.26 |
| WMD TOTAL 4 | 0.00 | 0.00 | 0.00 | 0.00 | 52.19 | 43,522.38 | 13,578,367.93 | 24,886.42 | 68,460.99 |
| LITCHFIELD WMD | | | | | | | | | |
| AITKIN | 0.00 | 0.00 | 0.00 | 0.00 | 0.00 | 69.86 | 28,000.00 | 0.00 | 69.86 |
| KANDIYOHI | 0.00 | 0.00 | 0.00 | 0.00 | 0.00 | 13,795.28 | 6,137,359.93 | 4,308.83 | 18,104.11 |
| MCLEOD | 0.00 | 0.00 | 0.00 | 0.00 | 0.00 | 1,224.85 | 1,737,790.00 | 797.27 | 2,022.12 |
| MEEKER | 0.00 | 0.00 | 0.00 | 0.00 | 0.00 | 4,866.29 | 4,157,389.90 | 2,441.37 | 7,307.66 |
| RENVILLE | 0.00 | 0.00 | 0.00 | 0.00 | 0.00 | 1,453.03 | 1,840,340.00 | 0.00 | 1,453.03 |
| STEARNS | 0.00 | 0.00 | 0.00 | 0.00 | 0.00 | 9,133.36 | 2,926,533.87 | 1,775.71 | 10,909.07 |
| TODD | 0.00 | 0.00 | 0.00 | 0.00 | 0.00 | 802.85 | 385,672.20 | 42.56 | 845.43 |
| WRIGHT | 0.00 | 0.00 | 0.00 | 0.00 | 0.00 | 2,791.57 | 4,333,820.90 | 437.50 | 3,229.07 |
| WMD TOTAL 8 | 0.00 | 0.00 | 0.00 | 0.00 | 0.00 | 34,137.09 | 21,546,868.00 | 9,803.26 | 43,940.35 |
| MINNESOTA VALLEY WMD | | | | | | | | | |
| BLUE EARTH | 0.00 | 0.00 | 0.00 | 0.00 | 0.00 | 1,234.92 | 1,741,450.00 | 454.61 | 1,689.53 |
| CARVER | 0.00 | 0.00 | 0.00 | 0.00 | 0.00 | 219.00 | 321,000.00 | 47.57 | 266.57 |
| DAKOTA | 0.00 | 0.00 | 0.00 | 0.00 | 0.00 | 73.90 | 201,747.00 | 0.05 | 73.95 |
| LESUEUR | 0.00 | 0.00 | 0.00 | 0.00 | 0.00 | 418.99 | 626,254.50 | 209.55 | 628.54 |
| RICE | 0.00 | 0.00 | 0.00 | 0.00 | 0.00 | 412.10 | 631,969.35 | 589.79 | 1,001.89 |
| SCOTT | 0.00 | 0.00 | 0.00 | 0.00 | 0.00 | 40.00 | 109,200.00 | 164.21 | 204.21 |
| SIBLEY | 0.00 | 0.00 | 0.00 | 0.00 | 43.48 | 862.40 | 1,079,789.75 | 253.25 | 1,159.13 |
| STEELE | 0.00 | 0.00 | 0.00 | 0.00 | 16.59 | 630.11 | 683,244.00 | 0.00 | 646.70 |
| WASECA | 0.00 | 0.00 | 0.00 | 0.00 | 0.00 | 248.78 | 408,000.00 | 0.00 | 248.78 |
| WMD TOTAL 9 | 0.00 | 0.00 | 0.00 | 0.00 | 60.07 | 4,140.20 | 5,772,684.58 | 1,718.63 | 5,918.90 |
| MORRIS WMD | | | | | | | | | |
| BIG STONE | 0.00 | 0.00 | 0.00 | 0.00 | 0.00 | 11,708.96 | 2,604,645.83 | 8,298.13 | 20,007.09 |
| CHIPPEWA | 0.00 | 0.00 | 0.00 | 0.00 | 5.00 | 244.12 | 127,050.00 | 110.10 | 359.20 |
| LAC QUI PARLE | 0.00 | 0.00 | 0.00 | 0.00 | 0.00 | 4,087.42 | 1,084,928.73 | 1,775.17 | 5,862.59 |
| POPE | 0.00 | 0.00 | 0.00 | 0.00 | 80.00 | 12,884.11 | 2,425,445.07 | 9,372.43 | 22,336.54 |
| STEVENS | 0.00 | 0.00 | 0.00 | 0.00 | 0.00 | 9,587.88 | 3,479,202.84 | 1,220.30 | 10,808.18 |
| SWIFT | 0.00 | 0.00 | 0.00 | 0.00 | 0.00 | 7,621.12 | 1,804,900.57 | 1,966.47 | 9,587.59 |
| TRAVERSE | 0.00 | 0.00 | 0.00 | 0.00 | 0.00 | 4,105.55 | 1,499,588.63 | 1,443.61 | 5,549.16 |
| YELLOW MEDICINE | 0.00 | 0.00 | 0.00 | 0.00 | 0.00 | 959.58 | 703,680.00 | 254.69 | 1,214.27 |
| WMD TOTAL 8 | 0.00 | 0.00 | 0.00 | 0.00 | 80.00 | 51,178.72 | 13,747,674.57 | 24,465.90 | 75,724.62 |
| TAMARAC WMD | | | | | | | | | |
| CASS | 0.00 | 0.00 | 0.00 | 0.00 | 0.00 | 0.00 | 0.00 | 43.00 | 43.00 |
| CLEARWATER | 0.00 | 0.00 | 0.00 | 0.00 | 0.00 | 0.00 | 0.00 | 864.00 | 864.00 |
| WMD TOTAL 2 | 0.00 | 0.00 | 0.00 | 0.00 | 0.00 | 0.00 | 0.00 | 907.00 | 907.00 |
| WINDOM WMD | | | | | | | | | |
| COTTONWOOD | 0.00 | 0.00 | 0.00 | 0.00 | 0.00 | 3,096.46 | 1,625,463.85 | 192.85 | 3,289.31 |
| FARIBAULT | 0.00 | 0.00 | 0.00 | 0.00 | 0.00 | 830.06 | 800,991.50 | 129.37 | 959.43 |
| FREEBORN | 0.00 | 0.00 | 0.00 | 0.00 | 133.61 | 1,695.82 | 2,014,017.25 | 543.26 | 1,972.69 |
| JACKSON | 0.00 | 0.00 | 0.00 | 0.00 | 0.00 | 4,480.47 | 3,593,810.29 | 380.09 | 4,860.56 |

TABLE 4 - WATERFOWL PRODUCTION AREAS

| STATE AND UNIT | RESERVED FROM PUBLIC DOMAIN | | ACQUIRED BY OTHER FEDERAL AGENCY | | DEVISE OR GIFT | PURCHASED | | AGREEMENT EASEMENT OR LEASE | TOTAL ACRES |
|---|---|---|---|---|---|---|---|---|---|
| | SOLE OR PRIMARY | SECONDARY | SOLE OR PRIMARY | SECONDARY | | ACRES | COST ($) | | |
| **MINNESOTA** | | | | | | | | | |
| WINDOM WMD | | | | | | | | | |
| MARTIN | 0.00 | 0.00 | 0.00 | 0.00 | 0.00 | 333.89 | 645,969.60 | 271.65 | 605.54 |
| MURRAY | 0.00 | 0.00 | 0.00 | 0.00 | 0.00 | 2,221.94 | 2,691,477.00 | 21.00 | 2,242.94 |
| NOBLES | 0.00 | 0.00 | 0.00 | 0.00 | 0.00 | 521.65 | 580,802.00 | 26.00 | 547.65 |
| ROCK | 0.00 | 0.00 | 0.00 | 0.00 | 0.00 | 0.00 | 0.00 | 11.00 | 11.00 |
| WATONWAN | 0.00 | 0.00 | 0.00 | 0.00 | 0.00 | 56.65 | 31,157.50 | 168.42 | 225.07 |
| WMD TOTAL 9 | 0.00 | 0.00 | 0.00 | 0.00 | 133.61 | 13,239.96 | 11,963,079.28 | 1,346.64 | 14,720.19 |
| STATE TOTAL 47 | 0.00 | 0.00 | 0.00 | 0.00 | 341.37 | 192,411.19 | 80,714,321.86 | 77,157.60 | 269,910.16 |
| **MONTANA** | | | | | | | | | |
| BENTON LAKE WMD | | | | | | | | | |
| CASCADE | 0.00 | 0.00 | 0.00 | 0.00 | 0.00 | 727.46 | 259,606.00 | 271.50 | 998.96 |
| CHOUTEAU | 0.00 | 0.00 | 0.00 | 0.00 | 0.00 | 2,136.13 | 538,543.00 | 781.00 | 2,917.13 |
| GLACIER | 0.00 | 0.00 | 0.00 | 0.00 | 0.00 | 94.20 | 17,898.00 | 10,243.33 | 10,337.53 |
| HILL | 0.00 | 0.00 | 0.00 | 0.00 | 378.93 | 0.00 | 0.00 | 918.00 | 1,296.93 |
| LEWIS AND CLARK | 0.00 | 0.00 | 0.00 | 0.00 | 0.00 | 0.00 | 0.00 | 5,989.95 | 5,989.95 |
| LIBERTY | 0.00 | 0.00 | 0.00 | 0.00 | 0.00 | 0.00 | 0.00 | 428.00 | 428.00 |
| PONDERA | 0.00 | 0.00 | 0.00 | 0.00 | 0.00 | 640.00 | 93,000.00 | 8,487.01 | 9,127.01 |
| POWELL | 0.00 | 0.00 | 0.00 | 0.00 | 1,802.07 | 2,752.60 | 1,053,804.00 | 24,268.32 | 28,822.99 |
| TETON | 0.00 | 0.00 | 0.00 | 0.00 | 0.00 | 1,486.05 | 376,253.00 | 6,296.37 | 7,782.42 |
| TOOLE | 0.00 | 0.00 | 0.00 | 0.00 | 0.00 | 4,610.48 | 1,003,964.00 | 12,166.37 | 16,776.85 |
| WMD TOTAL 10 | 0.00 | 0.00 | 0.00 | 0.00 | 2,181.00 | 12,446.92 | 3,383,068.00 | 69,849.85 | 84,477.77 |
| BOWDOIN WMD | | | | | | | | | |
| BLAINE | 0.00 | 0.00 | 0.00 | 0.00 | 0.00 | 2,436.26 | 167,340.00 | 10,724.20 | 13,159.46 |
| PHILLIPS | 0.00 | 0.00 | 0.00 | 0.00 | 51.00 | 6,877.83 | 1,371,863.00 | 30,413.36 | 37,342.19 |
| VALLEY | 0.00 | 0.00 | 0.00 | 0.00 | 0.00 | 0.00 | 0.00 | 201.00 | 201.00 |
| WMD TOTAL 3 | 0.00 | 0.00 | 0.00 | 0.00 | 51.00 | 9,313.09 | 1,539,203.00 | 41,338.56 | 50,702.65 |
| CHARLES M. RUSSELL WMD | | | | | | | | | |
| GOLDEN VALLEY | 0.00 | 0.00 | 0.00 | 0.00 | 0.00 | 760.27 | 76,427.00 | 160.00 | 920.27 |
| MUSSELSHELL | 0.00 | 0.00 | 0.00 | 0.00 | 0.00 | 532.45 | 165,001.00 | 160.00 | 692.45 |
| PETROLEUM | 0.00 | 0.00 | 0.00 | 0.00 | 0.00 | 40.00 | 23,800.00 | 0.00 | 40.00 |
| STILLWATER | 0.00 | 0.00 | 0.00 | 0.00 | 0.00 | 1,828.10 | 207,625.00 | 0.38 | 1,828.48 |
| YELLOWSTONE | 0.00 | 0.00 | 0.00 | 0.00 | 0.00 | 486.42 | 55,600.00 | 0.00 | 486.42 |
| WMD TOTAL 5 | 0.00 | 0.00 | 0.00 | 0.00 | 0.00 | 3,647.24 | 528,453.00 | 320.38 | 3,967.02 |
| NORTHEAST MONTANA WMD | | | | | | | | | |
| DANIELS | 0.00 | 0.00 | 0.00 | 0.00 | 7.85 | 1,080.58 | 87,669.00 | 1,011.32 | 2,099.75 |
| ROOSEVELT | 0.00 | 0.00 | 0.00 | 0.00 | 0.00 | 179.20 | 14,000.00 | 7,402.42 | 7,581.62 |
| SHERIDAN | 39.10 | 0.00 | 0.00 | 0.00 | 20.00 | 10,471.58 | 1,244,031.08 | 11,063.16 | 21,593.84 |
| WMD TOTAL 3 | 39.10 | 0.00 | 0.00 | 0.00 | 27.85 | 11,731.36 | 1,355,700.08 | 19,476.90 | 31,275.21 |
| NORTHWEST MONTANA WMD | | | | | | | | | |
| FLATHEAD | 0.00 | 0.00 | 0.00 | 0.00 | 807.92 | 4,410.31 | 2,246,518.00 | 0.00 | 5,218.23 |
| LAKE | 0.00 | 0.00 | 0.00 | 0.00 | 0.00 | 3,228.36 | 2,306,855.00 | 4,335.69 | 7,564.05 |
| WMD TOTAL 2 | 0.00 | 0.00 | 0.00 | 0.00 | 807.92 | 7,638.67 | 4,553,373.00 | 4,335.69 | 12,782.28 |
| STATE TOTAL 23 | 39.10 | 0.00 | 0.00 | 0.00 | 3,067.77 | 44,777.28 | 11,357,827.08 | 135,321.38 | 183,205.53 |
| **NEBRASKA** | | | | | | | | | |
| RAINWATER BASIN WMD | | | | | | | | | |
| ADAMS | 0.00 | 0.00 | 0.00 | 0.00 | 163.00 | 231.56 | 230,000.00 | 0.00 | 394.56 |
| CLAY | 0.00 | 0.00 | 1,092.19 | 0.00 | 260.00 | 5,028.14 | 2,346,258.85 | 4.25 | 6,384.58 |

TABLE 4 - WATERFOWL PRODUCTION AREAS

| STATE AND UNIT | | RESERVED FROM PUBLIC DOMAIN | | ACQUIRED BY OTHER FEDERAL AGENCY | | DEVISE OR GIFT | PURCHASED | | AGREEMENT EASEMENT OR LEASE | TOTAL ACRES |
|---|---|---|---|---|---|---|---|---|---|---|
| | | SOLE OR PRIMARY | SECONDARY | SOLE OR PRIMARY | SECONDARY | | ACRES | COST ($) | | |
| **NEBRASKA** | | | | | | | | | | |
| RAINWATER BASIN WMD | | | | | | | | | | |
| FILLMORE | | 0.00 | 0.00 | 0.00 | 0.00 | 0.00 | 3,337.60 | 1,631,453.00 | 6.60 | 3,344.20 |
| FRANKLIN | | 0.00 | 0.00 | 0.00 | 0.00 | 157.36 | 1,625.96 | 402,698.00 | 6.00 | 1,783.32 |
| GOSPER | | 0.00 | 0.00 | 0.00 | 0.00 | 0.00 | 1,451.50 | 233,923.00 | 0.00 | 1,451.50 |
| HALL | * | 0.00 | 0.00 | 320.70 | 0.00 | 0.00 | 328.77 | 433,000.00 | 0.00 | 649.47 |
| HAMILTON | * | 0.00 | 0.00 | 160.00 | 0.00 | 80.00 | 900.00 | 1,271,250.00 | 72.50 | 1,192.50 |
| KEARNEY | * | 0.00 | 0.00 | 0.00 | 0.00 | 0.00 | 2,874.43 | 657,621.00 | 175.50 | 3,049.93 |
| PHELPS | | 0.00 | 0.00 | 0.00 | 0.00 | 0.00 | 4,595.54 | 3,573,115.00 | 0.00 | 4,595.54 |
| POLK FSA | ** * | 0.00 | 0.00 | 0.00 | 0.00 | 0.00 | 0.00 | 0.00 | 140.75 | 140.75 |
| SALINE FSA | ** * | 0.00 | 0.00 | 61.35 | 0.00 | 0.00 | 0.00 | 0.00 | 43.00 | 104.35 |
| SEWARD | | 0.00 | 0.00 | 0.00 | 0.00 | 0.00 | 471.14 | 306,040.45 | 0.00 | 471.14 |
| YORK | * | 0.00 | 0.00 | 0.00 | 0.00 | 0.00 | 879.20 | 418,429.50 | 81.92 | 961.12 |
| WMD TOTAL | 11 | 0.00 | 0.00 | 1,594.24 | 0.00 | 680.36 | 21,703.44 | 11,509,814.30 | 524.56 | 24,502.59 |
| STATE TOTAL | 11 | 0.00 | 0.00 | 1,594.24 | 0.00 | 680.36 | 21,703.44 | 11,509,814.30 | 524.56 | 24,502.59 |
| **NORTH DAKOTA** | | | | | | | | | | |
| ARROWWOOD WMD | | | | | | | | | | |
| EDDY | * | 29.84 | 0.00 | 0.00 | 0.00 | 0.00 | 4,627.21 | 498,001.00 | 12,227.13 | 16,884.18 |
| FOSTER | | 0.00 | 0.00 | 0.00 | 0.00 | 0.00 | 1,487.07 | 96,568.00 | 6,828.00 | 8,315.07 |
| WMD TOTAL | 2 | 29.84 | 0.00 | 0.00 | 0.00 | 0.00 | 6,114.28 | 594,569.00 | 19,055.13 | 25,199.25 |
| AUDUBON WMD | | | | | | | | | | |
| HETTINGER | | 0.00 | 0.00 | 1,202.60 | 0.00 | 0.00 | 0.00 | 0.00 | 0.00 | 1,202.60 |
| MCLEAN | | 515.00 | 0.00 | 7,600.91 | 0.00 | 159.00 | 4,068.29 | 420,234.00 | 31,853.14 | 44,196.34 |
| SHERIDAN | * | 229.20 | 0.00 | 3,900.65 | 0.00 | 334.49 | 7,660.03 | 463,427.00 | 45,426.74 | 57,644.11 |
| WARD | | 120.00 | 0.00 | 0.00 | 0.00 | 0.00 | 5,868.60 | 486,211.00 | 47,943.89 | 53,932.49 |
| WMD TOTAL | 4 | 864.20 | 0.00 | 12,794.16 | 0.00 | 493.49 | 17,596.92 | 1,377,872.00 | 125,223.77 | 156,975.54 |
| CHASE LAKE PRAIRIE PROJECT WMD | | | | | | | | | | |
| STUTSMAN | * | 251.66 | 0.00 | 1,562.69 | 0.00 | 46.07 | 26,416.57 | 1,667,016.00 | 58,573.02 | 86,849.01 |
| WELLS | * | 0.00 | 0.00 | 2,935.40 | 0.00 | 0.00 | 7,661.43 | 1,188,569.00 | 13,928.40 | 24,525.23 |
| WMD TOTAL | 2 | 251.66 | 0.00 | 4,498.09 | 0.00 | 46.07 | 34,078.00 | 2,855,575.00 | 72,500.42 | 111,374.24 |
| CROSBY WMD | | | | | | | | | | |
| BURKE | | 0.00 | 0.00 | 0.00 | 0.00 | 0.00 | 3,544.19 | 180,068.00 | 45,148.54 | 48,680.73 |
| DIVIDE | | 1,244.83 | 0.00 | 0.00 | 0.00 | 0.00 | 9,444.62 | 474,790.00 | 36,581.95 | 47,271.40 |
| WILLIAMS | * | 320.00 | 0.00 | 0.00 | 0.00 | 0.00 | 4,163.17 | 278,057.00 | 8,640.00 | 13,123.17 |
| WMD TOTAL | 3 | 1,564.83 | 0.00 | 0.00 | 0.00 | 0.00 | 17,151.98 | 932,915.00 | 90,368.49 | 109,085.30 |
| DEVILS LAKE WMD | | | | | | | | | | |
| BENSON | * | 1,660.85 | 0.00 | 232.15 | 0.00 | 25.89 | 7,296.77 | 607,908.00 | 41,116.52 | 50,332.18 |
| CAVALIER | * | 0.00 | 0.00 | 723.71 | 0.00 | 0.00 | 10,129.12 | 1,364,471.00 | 13,910.00 | 24,762.83 |
| GRAND FORKS | | 18.30 | 0.00 | 0.00 | 0.00 | 21.77 | 6,766.72 | 1,462,108.85 | 1,505.90 | 8,312.69 |
| NELSON | * | 0.00 | 0.00 | 346.91 | 0.00 | 0.00 | 3,203.23 | 174,341.00 | 38,313.70 | 41,863.84 |
| PEMBINA | | 0.00 | 0.00 | 0.00 | 0.00 | 0.00 | 2,258.56 | 298,677.00 | 432.90 | 2,691.46 |
| RAMSEY | * | 132.10 | 0.00 | 1,119.43 | 0.00 | 41.96 | 8,163.04 | 1,144,252.00 | 29,116.00 | 38,562.53 |
| TOWNER | * | 13.50 | 0.00 | 829.39 | 0.00 | 1,281.05 | 5,117.02 | 902,146.00 | 25,554.37 | 32,795.33 |
| WALSH | * | 5.50 | 0.00 | 387.52 | 0.00 | 0.00 | 1,393.19 | 98,928.00 | 9,096.61 | 10,882.82 |
| WMD TOTAL | 8 | 1,830.25 | 0.00 | 3,603.11 | 0.00 | 1,370.67 | 44,347.65 | 5,962,031.85 | 159,052.00 | 210,233.68 |
| J. CLARK SALYER WMD | | | | | | | | | | |
| BOTTINEAU | * | 7.40 | 0.00 | 210.30 | 0.00 | 0.00 | 2,371.47 | 200,763.00 | 30,300.58 | 32,889.75 |
| MCHENRY | * | 993.59 | 0.00 | 0.00 | 0.00 | 0.00 | 4,888.80 | 376,404.50 | 52,863.27 | 58,745.66 |
| PIERCE | * | 3,276.00 | 0.00 | 1,054.56 | 0.00 | 12.68 | 5,406.26 | 922,056.00 | 43,799.61 | 54,549.11 |

TABLE 4 - WATERFOWL PRODUCTION AREAS

| STATE AND UNIT | | RESERVED FROM PUBLIC DOMAIN | | ACQUIRED BY OTHER FEDERAL AGENCY | | DEVISE OR GIFT | PURCHASED | | | TOTAL ACRES |
|---|---|---|---|---|---|---|---|---|---|---|
| | | SOLE OR PRIMARY | SECONDARY | SOLE OR PRIMARY | SECONDARY | | ACRES | COST ($) | AGREEMENT EASEMENT OR LEASE | |
| **NORTH DAKOTA** | | | | | | | | | | |
| J. CLARK SALYER WMD | | | | | | | | | | |
| RENVILLE | | 0.00 | 0.00 | 0.00 | 0.00 | 0.00 | 311.09 | 20,523.00 | 16,766.60 | 37,078.69 |
| ROLETTE | | 105.96 | 0.00 | 0.00 | 0.00 | 0.00 | 5,694.03 | 759,347.00 | 20,510.01 | 36,310.00 |
| WMD TOTAL | 5 | 4,382.95 | 0.00 | 1,264.86 | 0.00 | 12.68 | 21,671.65 | 2,280,092.50 | 162,239.07 | 189,571.21 |
| KULM WMD | | | | | | | | | | |
| DICKEY | * | 306.75 | 0.00 | 0.00 | 0.00 | 0.00 | 9,735.40 | 1,150,816.00 | 42,394.61 | 52,436.56 |
| LA MOURE | * | 0.00 | 0.00 | 634.89 | 0.00 | 0.00 | 4,799.96 | 505,095.00 | 15,202.70 | 20,637.55 |
| LOGAN | * | 835.00 | 0.00 | 160.03 | 0.00 | 0.00 | 11,226.24 | 1,006,598.00 | 52,180.96 | 64,402.23 |
| MCINTOSH | * | 297.58 | 0.00 | 0.00 | 0.00 | 9.60 | 17,373.48 | 1,368,865.00 | 34,657.32 | 52,337.98 |
| WMD TOTAL | 4 | 1,439.33 | 0.00 | 794.92 | 0.00 | 9.60 | 43,135.08 | 4,031,374.00 | 144,436.49 | 189,814.42 |
| LONG LAKE WMD | | | | | | | | | | |
| BURLEIGH | * | 850.10 | 0.00 | 794.69 | 0.00 | 0.00 | 9,615.44 | 1,949,864.00 | 50,359.57 | 61,616.20 |
| EMMONS | * | 480.00 | 0.00 | 0.00 | 0.00 | 0.00 | 3,135.29 | 174,321.75 | 11,800.60 | 15,415.89 |
| KIDDER | * | 1,769.79 | 0.00 | 0.00 | 0.00 | 66.36 | 5,547.52 | 438,439.00 | 83,178.90 | 96,582.57 |
| WMD TOTAL | 3 | 3,099.89 | 0.00 | 794.69 | 0.00 | 66.36 | 18,294.25 | 2,562,624.75 | 151,339.47 | 173,614.66 |
| LOSTWOOD WMD | | | | | | | | | | |
| MOUNTRAIL | * | 467.52 | 0.00 | 400.00 | 0.00 | 250.00 | 9,905.10 | 940,661.00 | 60,610.78 | 71,633.40 |
| WMD TOTAL | 1 | 467.52 | 0.00 | 400.00 | 0.00 | 250.00 | 9,905.10 | 940,661.00 | 60,610.78 | 71,633.40 |
| TEWAUKON WMD | | | | | | | | | | |
| RANSOM | | 0.00 | 0.00 | 0.00 | 0.00 | 0.00 | 4,315.02 | 617,357.00 | 23,831.48 | 28,146.50 |
| RICHLAND | | 0.00 | 0.00 | 0.00 | 0.00 | 0.00 | 6,072.25 | 986,052.00 | 7,060.12 | 13,132.37 |
| SARGENT | * | 0.00 | 0.00 | 405.71 | 0.00 | 0.00 | 3,537.46 | 305,439.00 | 21,355.08 | 25,298.25 |
| WMD TOTAL | 3 | 0.00 | 0.00 | 405.71 | 0.00 | 0.00 | 13,924.73 | 1,908,848.00 | 52,246.68 | 66,577.12 |
| VALLEY CITY WMD | | | | | | | | | | |
| BARNES | * | 1.26 | 0.00 | 338.63 | 0.00 | 15.61 | 6,661.68 | 958,087.00 | 20,388.50 | 27,405.68 |
| CASS | | 0.00 | 0.00 | 0.00 | 0.00 | 0.00 | 3,439.89 | 628,344.00 | 1,759.90 | 5,199.79 |
| GRIGGS | | 158.05 | 0.00 | 0.00 | 0.00 | 0.00 | 3,060.46 | 373,990.00 | 16,776.20 | 20,005.71 |
| STEELE | | 0.00 | 0.00 | 0.00 | 0.00 | 0.00 | 3,249.25 | 536,345.00 | 4,404.30 | 7,653.55 |
| TRAILL | | 0.00 | 0.00 | 0.00 | 0.00 | 0.00 | 719.25 | 75,109.00 | 234.00 | 953.25 |
| WMD TOTAL | 5 | 159.31 | 0.00 | 338.63 | 0.00 | 15.61 | 17,139.53 | 2,573,875.00 | 43,564.90 | 61,217.98 |
| STATE TOTAL | 40 | 14,089.78 | 0.00 | 24,924.17 | 0.00 | 2,284.48 | 243,362.17 | 26,020,438.10 | 1,080,636.20 | 1,365,296.80 |
| **SOUTH DAKOTA** | | | | | | | | | | |
| HURON WMD | | | | | | | | | | |
| BEADLE | * | 0.00 | 0.00 | 240.00 | 0.00 | 70.19 | 7,256.45 | 1,651,212.69 | 44,184.99 | 51,751.63 |
| BUFFALO | | 0.00 | 0.00 | 0.00 | 0.00 | 916.52 | 0.00 | 0.00 | 1,343.61 | 2,260.13 |
| HAND | * | 80.00 | 0.00 | 0.00 | 0.00 | 239.00 | 3,671.31 | 680,280.35 | 62,452.17 | 66,442.48 |
| HUGHES | | 0.00 | 0.00 | 0.00 | 0.00 | 0.00 | 455.99 | 82,800.00 | 3,265.09 | 3,721.08 |
| HYDE | * | 0.00 | 0.00 | 0.00 | 0.00 | 2,401.36 | 0.00 | 0.00 | 39,755.64 | 42,157.00 |
| JERAULD | * | 40.00 | 0.00 | 0.00 | 0.00 | 320.00 | 1,430.40 | 217,041.00 | 24,268.65 | 26,059.05 |
| SANBORN | * | 0.00 | 0.00 | 0.00 | 0.00 | 0.00 | 93.00 | 5,250.00 | 38,898.67 | 38,991.67 |
| SULLY | * | 0.00 | 0.00 | 0.00 | 0.00 | 0.00 | 266.48 | 9,993.00 | 4,449.51 | 4,715.99 |
| WMD TOTAL | 8 | 120.00 | 0.00 | 240.00 | 0.00 | 3,947.07 | 13,173.63 | 2,546,557.04 | 218,618.33 | 236,096.03 |
| LACREEK WMD | | | | | | | | | | |
| HAAKON FSA | ** * | 0.00 | 0.00 | 0.00 | 0.00 | 0.00 | 0.00 | 0.00 | 1,806.10 | 1,806.10 |
| JONES FSA | ** * | 0.00 | 0.00 | 0.00 | 0.00 | 0.00 | 0.00 | 0.00 | 232.00 | 232.00 |
| STANLEY FSA | ** * | 0.00 | 0.00 | 0.00 | 0.00 | 0.00 | 0.00 | 0.00 | 1,431.40 | 1,431.40 |
| WMD TOTAL | 0 | 0.00 | 0.00 | 0.00 | 0.00 | 0.00 | 0.00 | 0.00 | 3,469.50 | 3,469.50 |

TABLE 4 - WATERFOWL PRODUCTION AREAS

| STATE AND UNIT | | RESERVED FROM PUBLIC DOMAIN | | ACQUIRED BY OTHER FEDERAL AGENCY | | DEVISE OR GIFT | PURCHASED | | AGREEMENT EASEMENT OR LEASE | TOTAL ACRES |
|---|---|---|---|---|---|---|---|---|---|---|
| | | SOLE OR PRIMARY | SECONDARY | SOLE OR PRIMARY | SECONDARY | | ACRES | COST ($) | | |
| **SOUTH DAKOTA** | | | | | | | | | | |
| LAKE ANDES WMD | | | | | | | | | | |
| AURORA | * | 0.00 | 0.00 | 0.00 | 0.00 | 0.00 | 4,716.08 | 822,316.00 | 36,058.98 | 40,775.06 |
| BON HOMME | * | 0.00 | 0.00 | 0.00 | 0.00 | 0.00 | 1,174.17 | 303,624.90 | 252.79 | 1,426.90 |
| BRULE | | 0.00 | 0.00 | 0.00 | 0.00 | 0.00 | 1,074.13 | 89,404.00 | 19,625.69 | 20,699.82 |
| CHARLES MIX | * | 0.00 | 0.00 | 0.00 | 0.00 | 285.70 | 4,110.82 | 1,172,947.00 | 8,949.37 | 13,345.89 |
| CLAY | * | 0.00 | 0.00 | 0.00 | 0.00 | 0.00 | 40.00 | 8,000.00 | 59.50 | 99.50 |
| DAVISON | * | 0.00 | 0.00 | 0.00 | 0.00 | 0.00 | 229.92 | 24,340.00 | 354.10 | 584.02 |
| DOUGLAS | * | 0.00 | 0.00 | 0.00 | 0.00 | 449.73 | 3,852.05 | 647,691.00 | 4,076.40 | 8,378.18 |
| HANSON | * | 0.00 | 0.00 | 0.00 | 0.00 | 0.00 | 1,075.60 | 285,803.00 | 2,813.28 | 3,888.88 |
| HUTCHINSON | * | 0.00 | 0.00 | 0.00 | 0.00 | 0.00 | 789.51 | 227,646.25 | 1,229.50 | 2,079.01 |
| LINCOLN | | 0.00 | 0.00 | 0.00 | 0.00 | 0.00 | 177.22 | 39,905.00 | 300.50 | 477.72 |
| TRIPP FSA | ** * | 0.00 | 0.00 | 0.00 | 0.00 | 0.00 | 0.00 | 0.00 | 5.90 | 5.90 |
| TURNER | * | 0.00 | 0.00 | 0.00 | 0.00 | 0.00 | 850.09 | 430,044.90 | 479.90 | 1,329.99 |
| UNION | | 0.00 | 0.00 | 0.00 | 0.00 | 0.00 | 98.02 | 23,301.00 | 0.00 | 98.02 |
| YANKTON | | 0.00 | 0.00 | 0.00 | 0.00 | 0.00 | 294.63 | 129,592.00 | 488.60 | 783.23 |
| WMD TOTAL | 13 | 0.00 | 0.00 | 0.00 | 0.00 | 735.43 | 58,480.24 | 4,008,085.05 | 74,694.45 | 93,910.12 |
| MADISON WMD | | | | | | | | | | |
| BROOKINGS | * | 0.00 | 0.00 | 0.00 | 0.00 | 158.25 | 6,075.80 | 1,430,276.70 | 6,622.86 | 14,806.91 |
| DEUEL | * | 0.00 | 0.00 | 0.00 | 0.00 | 0.00 | 3,209.87 | 481,522.00 | 27,271.23 | 30,480.10 |
| HAMLIN | * | 0.00 | 0.00 | 0.00 | 0.00 | 0.00 | 3,400.89 | 954,563.00 | 6,319.14 | 9,720.03 |
| KINGSBURY | * | 0.00 | 0.00 | 0.00 | 0.00 | 0.00 | 6,924.04 | 1,838,680.80 | 26,116.58 | 33,040.92 |
| LAKE | * | 0.00 | 0.00 | 0.00 | 0.00 | 359.34 | 5,744.07 | 1,308,607.75 | 7,019.22 | 13,122.63 |
| MCCOOK | * | 0.00 | 0.00 | 0.00 | 0.00 | 0.00 | 3,362.96 | 680,843.90 | 7,151.87 | 10,514.83 |
| MINER | * | 40.00 | 0.00 | 0.00 | 0.00 | 0.00 | 1,545.87 | 153,695.00 | 25,382.74 | 26,968.61 |
| MINNEHAHA | * | 0.00 | 0.00 | 0.00 | 0.00 | 0.00 | 4,406.62 | 1,100,295.00 | 1,850.96 | 6,150.59 |
| MOODY | * | 0.00 | 0.00 | 0.00 | 0.00 | 277.22 | 2,903.78 | 927,478.85 | 2,387.69 | 5,568.69 |
| WMD TOTAL | 9 | 40.00 | 0.00 | 0.00 | 0.00 | 794.81 | 37,605.91 | 8,873,964.70 | 111,922.59 | 150,423.31 |
| SAND LAKE WMD | | | | | | | | | | |
| BROWN | * | 0.00 | 0.00 | 0.00 | 0.00 | 482.62 | 4,094.60 | 819,223.80 | 51,689.98 | 56,267.20 |
| CAMPBELL | | 240.00 | 0.00 | 0.00 | 0.00 | 0.00 | 1,919.71 | 186,548.00 | 22,497.15 | 24,656.86 |
| CORSON FSA | ** * | 0.00 | 0.00 | 0.00 | 0.00 | 0.00 | 0.00 | 0.00 | 1,105.90 | 1,105.90 |
| DEWEY FSA | ** * | 0.00 | 0.00 | 0.00 | 0.00 | 0.00 | 0.00 | 0.00 | 2,361.80 | 2,361.80 |
| EDMUNDS | * | 0.00 | 0.00 | 0.00 | 0.00 | 760.00 | 9,905.76 | 3,717,204.00 | 121,234.79 | 132,360.55 |
| FAULK | * | 0.00 | 0.00 | 0.00 | 0.00 | 0.00 | 2,508.88 | 480,998.00 | 133,776.99 | 136,283.87 |
| MCPHERSON | * | 180.45 | 0.00 | 0.00 | 0.00 | 1,381.23 | 19,414.42 | 3,396,800.80 | 148,629.36 | 169,605.46 |
| POTTER | * | 0.00 | 0.00 | 0.00 | 0.00 | 0.00 | 682.63 | 71,179.00 | 23,673.83 | 24,356.46 |
| SPINK | * | 520.00 | 0.00 | 0.00 | 0.00 | 200.00 | 2,226.43 | 388,890.00 | 27,727.15 | 30,673.58 |
| WALWORTH | * | 335.71 | 0.00 | 0.00 | 0.00 | 0.00 | 1,524.54 | 193,800.00 | 19,402.07 | 21,262.32 |
| WMD TOTAL | 8 | 1,256.16 | 0.00 | 0.00 | 0.00 | 2,223.85 | 41,365.30 | 7,254,220.60 | 554,058.69 | 598,904.00 |
| WAUBAY WMD | | | | | | | | | | |
| CLARK | * | 95.75 | 0.00 | 0.00 | 0.00 | 0.00 | 6,033.11 | 843,303.90 | 46,707.56 | 52,836.40 |
| CODINGTON | * | 31.23 | 0.00 | 0.00 | 0.00 | 1,188.42 | 5,089.31 | 882,837.70 | 11,075.65 | 17,384.61 |
| DAY | | 208.75 | 0.00 | 0.00 | 0.00 | 0.00 | 6,411.50 | 486,566.00 | 46,197.94 | 52,818.19 |
| GRANT | | 0.00 | 0.00 | 0.00 | 0.00 | 0.00 | 5,362.99 | 1,005,000.00 | 20,770.42 | 26,133.41 |
| MARSHALL | * | 96.89 | 0.00 | 0.00 | 0.00 | 671.23 | 10,218.51 | 1,561,629.00 | 57,335.18 | 68,311.81 |
| ROBERTS | * | 0.00 | 0.00 | 0.00 | 0.00 | 0.00 | 5,032.73 | 625,710.80 | 51,997.34 | 57,030.07 |
| WMD TOTAL | 6 | 352.60 | 0.00 | 0.00 | 0.00 | 1,659.65 | 38,148.15 | 5,775,747.40 | 234,354.09 | 274,514.49 |
| STATE TOTAL | 44 | 1,768.76 | 0.00 | 240.00 | 0.00 | 9,360.81 | 148,633.23 | 28,498,574.79 | 1,197,117.65 | 1,357,320.45 |
| **WISCONSIN** | | | | | | | | | | |
| LEOPOLD WMD | | | | | | | | | | |
| ADAMS | | 0.00 | 0.00 | 0.00 | 0.00 | 0.00 | 344.00 | 172,500.00 | 0.00 | 344.00 |

TABLE 4 - WATERFOWL PRODUCTION AREAS

| STATE AND UNIT | | RESERVED FROM PUBLIC DOMAIN | | ACQUIRED BY OTHER FEDERAL AGENCY | | DEVISE OR GIFT | PURCHASED | | AGREEMENT EASEMENT OR LEASE | TOTAL ACRES |
|---|---|---|---|---|---|---|---|---|---|---|
| | | SOLE OR PRIMARY | SECONDARY | SOLE OR PRIMARY | SECONDARY | | ACRES | COST ($) | | |
| **WISCONSIN** | | | | | | | | | | |
| LEOPOLD WMD | | | | | | | | | | |
| COLUMBIA | | 0.00 | 0.00 | 0.00 | 0.00 | 26.00 | 3,365.63 | 3,573,816.45 | 0.00 | 3,391.63 |
| DANE | | 0.00 | 0.00 | 0.00 | 0.00 | 0.00 | 1,591.08 | 2,109,875.65 | 0.00 | 1,591.08 |
| DODGE | | 0.00 | 0.00 | 0.00 | 0.00 | 0.00 | 726.97 | 967,652.33 | 0.43 | 727.40 |
| FOND DU LAC | | 0.00 | 0.00 | 0.00 | 0.00 | 0.00 | 949.36 | 1,196,452.00 | 0.00 | 949.36 |
| JEFFERSON | | 0.00 | 0.00 | 0.00 | 0.00 | 0.00 | 249.79 | 241,239.00 | 0.00 | 249.79 |
| MANITOWOC | | 0.00 | 0.00 | 0.00 | 0.00 | 0.00 | 120.00 | 66,000.00 | 0.00 | 120.00 |
| MARQUETTE | | 0.00 | 0.00 | 0.00 | 0.00 | 0.00 | 259.97 | 119,480.00 | 0.00 | 259.97 |
| OZAUKEE | | 0.00 | 0.00 | 0.00 | 0.00 | 0.00 | 536.30 | 679,413.40 | 0.00 | 536.30 |
| ROCK | | 0.00 | 0.00 | 0.00 | 0.00 | 0.00 | 349.32 | 302,358.71 | 0.00 | 349.32 |
| SAUK | | 0.00 | 0.00 | 0.00 | 0.00 | 0.00 | 210.88 | 538,000.00 | 0.00 | 210.88 |
| SHEBOYGAN | | 0.00 | 0.00 | 0.00 | 0.00 | 0.00 | 709.91 | 1,639,638.94 | 0.00 | 709.91 |
| WAUSHARA | | 0.00 | 0.00 | 0.00 | 0.00 | 0.00 | 232.30 | 243,000.00 | 0.00 | 232.30 |
| WINNEBAGO | | 0.00 | 0.00 | 0.00 | 0.00 | 0.00 | 1,918.27 | 1,331,300.00 | 0.00 | 1,918.27 |
| WMD TOTAL | 14 | 0.00 | 0.00 | 0.00 | 0.00 | 26.00 | 11,563.78 | 13,172,726.48 | 0.43 | 11,590.21 |
| ST. CROIX WMD | | | | | | | | | | |
| DUNN | | 0.00 | 0.00 | 0.00 | 0.00 | 0.00 | 621.98 | 698,200.00 | 0.00 | 621.98 |
| POLK | | 0.00 | 0.00 | 0.00 | 0.00 | 0.00 | 1,045.07 | 509,094.00 | 0.00 | 1,045.07 |
| ST. CROIX | | 0.00 | 0.00 | 0.00 | 0.00 | 0.00 | 5,444.67 | 7,196,004.56 | 1.64 | 5,446.31 |
| WMD TOTAL | 3 | 0.00 | 0.00 | 0.00 | 0.00 | 0.00 | 7,111.72 | 8,403,298.56 | 1.64 | 7,113.36 |
| STATE TOTAL | 17 | 0.00 | 0.00 | 0.00 | 0.00 | 26.00 | 18,675.50 | 21,576,025.04 | 2.07 | 18,703.57 |
| GRAND TOTAL | 204 | 15,897.64 | 0.00 | 26,756.41 | 0.00 | 15,899.85 | 895,476.77 | 213,340,208.99 | 2,491,397.15 | 3,246,429.82 |

\* - COUNTY WHERE WPA PROGRAM CURRENTLY EXISTS AND NEW FSA INTERESTS ARE ACQUIRED.
\*\* - SUMMARY BY COUNTY OF ALL OTHER ACRES, BOTH FEE AND LESS THAN FEE, ACQUIRED FROM
   THE FSA, NOT REPORTED WITHIN AN EXISTING PROJECT. SUMMARY MAY CONTAIN ONE OR MORE
   OWNERSHIPS. FSA COUNTY SUMMARY ACRES ARE INCLUDED IN THE TOTAL ACRES FOR EACH
   STATE BUT ARE NOT SEPARATE UNITS IN THE WATERFOWL PRODUCTION AREA STATE TOTALS.

WMD - WETLANDS MANAGEMENT DISTRICT
FSA - FARM SERVICE AGENCY (FORMERLY FARMERS HOME ADMINISTRATION, DEPARTMENT OF
   AGRICULTURE)

TABLE 5 - COORDINATION AREAS

| STATE AND UNIT | | RESERVED FROM PUBLIC DOMAIN | | ACQUIRED BY OTHER FEDERAL AGENCY | | DEVISE OR GIFT | PURCHASED | | AGREEMENT EASEMENT OR LEASE | TOTAL ACRES |
|---|---|---|---|---|---|---|---|---|---|---|
| | | SOLE OR PRIMARY | SECONDARY | SOLE OR PRIMARY | SECONDARY | | ACRES | COST ($) | | |
| **ARIZONA** | | | | | | | | | | |
| GILA RIVER | | 6,896.54 | 0.00 | 0.00 | 0.00 | 0.00 | 0.00 | 0.00 | 0.00 | 6,896.54 |
| STATE TOTAL | 1 | 6,896.54 | 0.00 | 0.00 | 0.00 | 0.00 | 0.00 | 0.00 | 0.00 | 6,896.54 |
| **CALIFORNIA** | | | | | | | | | | |
| HONEY LAKE | | 1,050.29 | 0.00 | 0.00 | 0.00 | 0.00 | 0.00 | 0.00 | 0.00 | 1,050.29 |
| TOPAZ LAKE | | 200.00 | 0.00 | 0.00 | 0.00 | 0.00 | 0.00 | 0.00 | 0.00 | 200.00 |
| STATE TOTAL | 2 | 1,250.29 | 0.00 | 0.00 | 0.00 | 0.00 | 0.00 | 0.00 | 0.00 | 1,250.29 |
| **COLORADO** | | | | | | | | | | |
| HOT SULPHUR | | 1,115.00 | 0.00 | 0.00 | 0.00 | 0.00 | 0.00 | 0.00 | 0.00 | 1,115.00 |
| MACK MESA | | 37.53 | 0.00 | 0.00 | 0.00 | 0.00 | 0.00 | 0.00 | 0.00 | 37.53 |
| STATE TOTAL | 2 | 1,152.53 | 0.00 | 0.00 | 0.00 | 0.00 | 0.00 | 0.00 | 0.00 | 1,152.53 |
| **IDAHO** | | | | | | | | | | |
| C. J. STRIKE | | 1,544.90 | 0.00 | 0.00 | 0.00 | 0.00 | 0.00 | 0.00 | 0.00 | 1,544.90 |
| CAREY LAKE | | 320.00 | 0.00 | 0.00 | 0.00 | 0.00 | 0.00 | 0.00 | 0.00 | 320.00 |
| HAGERMAN | | 0.00 | 0.00 | 0.00 | 0.00 | 0.00 | 219.78 | 13,070.00 | 0.00 | 219.78 |
| NORTH LAKE | | 2,705.32 | 0.00 | 0.00 | 0.00 | 0.00 | 0.00 | 0.00 | 0.00 | 2,705.32 |
| SAND CREEK | | 1,000.00 | 0.00 | 0.00 | 0.00 | 0.00 | 0.00 | 0.00 | 0.00 | 1,000.00 |
| STATE TOTAL | 5 | 5,570.22 | 0.00 | 0.00 | 0.00 | 0.00 | 219.78 | 13,070.00 | 0.00 | 5,790.00 |
| **ILLINOIS** | | | | | | | | | | |
| MISSISSIPPI RIVER | | 0.00 | 0.00 | 0.00 E | 26,626.00 | 0.00 | 0.00 | 0.00 | 0.00 | 26,626.00 |
| STATE TOTAL | 1 | 0.00 | 0.00 | 0.00 | 26,626.00 | 0.00 | 0.00 | 0.00 | 0.00 | 26,626.00 |
| **IOWA** | | | | | | | | | | |
| GREEN ISLAND | | 0.00 | 0.00 | 0.00 E | 2,571.00 | 0.00 | 82.00 | 410.00 | 0.00 | 2,653.00 |
| LAKE ODESSA | | 0.00 | 0.00 | 0.00 E | 3,134.00 | 0.00 | 0.00 | 0.00 | 0.00 | 3,134.00 |
| PRINCETON | | 0.00 | 0.00 | 0.00 E | 794.00 | 0.00 | 0.00 | 0.00 | 0.00 | 794.00 |
| STATE TOTAL | 3 | 0.00 | 0.00 | 0.00 | 6,499.00 | 0.00 | 82.00 | 410.00 | 0.00 | 6,581.00 |
| **MINNESOTA** | | | | | | | | | | |
| BELTRAMI | | 0.00 | 0.00 | 81,651.38 | 0.00 | 0.00 | 0.00 | 0.00 | 0.00 | 81,651.38 |
| PIPESTONE | | 0.00 | 0.00 | 117.72 | 0.00 | 0.00 | 0.00 | 0.00 | 0.00 | 117.72 |
| STATE TOTAL | 2 | 0.00 | 0.00 | 81,769.10 | 0.00 | 0.00 | 0.00 | 0.00 | 0.00 | 81,769.10 |
| **MISSOURI** | | | | | | | | | | |
| CLARKSVILLE | | 0.00 | 0.00 | 0.00 E | 282.00 | 0.00 | 0.00 | 0.00 | 0.00 | 282.00 |
| ELSBERRY | | 0.00 | 0.00 | 0.00 E | 1,286.00 | 0.00 | 0.00 | 0.00 | 0.00 | 1,286.00 |
| MISSISSIPPI RIVER | | 0.00 | 0.00 | 0.00 E | 10,265.00 | 0.00 | 0.00 | 0.00 | 0.00 | 10,265.00 |
| WEST QUINCY | | 0.00 | 0.00 | 0.00 E | 242.00 | 0.00 | 0.00 | 0.00 | 0.00 | 242.00 |
| STATE TOTAL | 4 | 0.00 | 0.00 | 0.00 | 12,075.00 | 0.00 | 0.00 | 0.00 | 0.00 | 12,075.00 |
| **MONTANA** | | | | | | | | | | |
| BULL MOUNTAIN | | 1,599.32 | 0.00 | 0.00 | 0.00 | 0.00 | 0.00 | 0.00 | 0.00 | 1,599.32 |
| DODSON | | 120.00 | 0.00 | 0.00 | 0.00 | 0.00 | 0.00 | 0.00 | 0.00 | 120.00 |
| FOX LAKE | | 160.00 | 0.00 | 0.00 | 0.00 | 0.00 | 0.00 | 0.00 | 0.00 | 160.00 |
| FREEZEOUT LAKE | | 434.80 | 0.00 | 0.00 | 0.00 | 0.00 | 0.00 | 0.00 | 0.00 | 434.80 |
| JUDITH RIVER | | 234.49 | 0.00 | 0.00 | 0.00 | 0.00 | 0.00 | 0.00 | 0.00 | 234.49 |
| SUN RIVER | | 4,144.83 | 0.00 | 0.00 | 0.00 | 0.00 | 0.00 | 0.00 | 0.00 | 4,144.83 |
| STATE TOTAL | 6 | 6,693.44 | 0.00 | 0.00 | 0.00 | 0.00 | 0.00 | 0.00 | 0.00 | 6,693.44 |
| **NEVADA** | | | | | | | | | | |
| STILLWATER | | 0.00 | 0.00 | 0.00 | 0.00 | 0.00 | 0.00 | 0.00 | 63,544.00 | 63,544.00 |
| STATE TOTAL | 1 | 0.00 | 0.00 | 0.00 | 0.00 | 0.00 | 0.00 | 0.00 | 63,544.00 | 63,544.00 |

TABLE 5 - COORDINATION AREAS

| STATE AND UNIT | | RESERVED FROM PUBLIC DOMAIN | | ACQUIRED BY OTHER FEDERAL AGENCY | | DEVISE OR GIFT | PURCHASED | | AGREEMENT EASEMENT OR LEASE | TOTAL ACRES |
|---|---|---|---|---|---|---|---|---|---|---|
| | | SOLE OR PRIMARY | SECONDARY | SOLE OR PRIMARY | SECONDARY | | ACRES | COST ($) | | |
| **NEW YORK** | | | | | | | | | | |
| LIDO BEACH | | 0.00 | 0.00 | 22.42 | 0.00 | 0.00 | 0.00 | 0.00 | 0.00 | 22.42 |
| STATE TOTAL | 1 | 0.00 | 0.00 | 22.42 | 0.00 | 0.00 | 0.00 | 0.00 | 0.00 | 22.42 |
| **NORTH DAKOTA** | | | | | | | | | | |
| LAKE WASHINGTON | | 3.68 | 0.00 | 0.00 | 0.00 | 0.00 | 0.00 | 0.00 | 0.00 | 3.68 |
| STATE TOTAL | 1 | 3.68 | 0.00 | 0.00 | 0.00 | 0.00 | 0.00 | 0.00 | 0.00 | 3.68 |
| **OREGON** | | | | | | | | | | |
| GOVERNMENT ISLAND | | 1.79 | 0.00 | 0.00 | 0.00 | 0.00 | 0.00 | 0.00 | 0.00 | 1.79 |
| OCHOCO RESERVOIR | | 40.00 | 0.00 | 0.00 | 0.00 | 0.00 | 0.00 | 0.00 | 0.00 | 40.00 |
| SUMMER LAKE | | 7,127.65 | 0.00 | 0.00 | 0.00 | 0.00 | 0.00 | 0.00 | 0.00 | 7,127.65 |
| STATE TOTAL | 3 | 7,169.44 | 0.00 | 0.00 | 0.00 | 0.00 | 0.00 | 0.00 | 0.00 | 7,169.44 |
| **UTAH** | | | | | | | | | | |
| DESERT LAKES | | 880.00 | 0.00 | 1,741.23 | 0.00 | 0.00 | 0.00 | 0.00 | 0.00 | 2,621.23 |
| ROCK ISLAND | | 1.74 | 0.00 | 0.00 | 0.00 | 0.00 | 0.00 | 0.00 | 0.00 | 1.74 |
| TOPAZ LAKE | | 3,662.13 | 0.00 | 480.00 | 0.00 | 0.00 | 0.00 | 0.00 | 0.00 | 4,142.13 |
| STATE TOTAL | 3 | 4,543.87 | 0.00 | 2,221.23 | 0.00 | 0.00 | 0.00 | 0.00 | 0.00 | 6,765.10 |
| **WASHINGTON** | | | | | | | | | | |
| COLOCKUM | | 4,957.23 | 0.00 | 0.00 | 0.00 | 0.00 | 0.00 | 0.00 | 0.00 | 4,957.23 |
| LENORE | | 5,787.00 | 0.00 | 0.00 | 0.00 | 0.00 | 0.00 | 0.00 | 0.00 | 5,787.00 |
| MARROWSTONE | | 56.25 | 0.00 | 0.00 | 0.00 | 0.00 | 0.00 | 0.00 | 0.00 | 56.25 |
| METHOW | | 3,037.97 | 0.00 | 0.00 | 0.00 | 0.00 | 0.00 | 0.00 | 0.00 | 3,037.97 |
| PHALON LAKE | | 9.70 | 0.00 | 0.00 | 0.00 | 0.00 | 0.00 | 0.00 | 0.00 | 9.70 |
| SHERMAN CREEK | | 560.00 | 0.00 | 0.00 | 0.00 | 0.00 | 0.00 | 0.00 | 0.00 | 560.00 |
| SINLAHEKIN | | 2,803.83 | 0.00 | 0.00 | 0.00 | 0.00 | 0.00 | 0.00 | 0.00 | 2,803.83 |
| SUNNYSIDE | | 320.00 | 0.00 | 0.00 | 0.00 | 0.00 | 0.00 | 0.00 | 0.00 | 320.00 |
| STATE TOTAL | 8 | 17,521.98 | 0.00 | 0.00 | 0.00 | 0.00 | 0.00 | 0.00 | 0.00 | 17,521.98 |
| **WISCONSIN** | | | | | | | | | | |
| NECEDAH | | 33.18 | 0.00 | 55,260.72 | 0.00 | 0.00 | 379.35 | 0.00 | 0.00 | 55,673.25 |
| STATE TOTAL | 1 | 33.18 | 0.00 | 55,260.72 | 0.00 | 0.00 | 379.35 | 0.00 | 0.00 | 55,673.25 |
| **WYOMING** | | | | | | | | | | |
| EAST FORK | | 3,432.04 | 0.00 | 0.00 | 0.00 | 0.00 | 0.00 | 0.00 | 0.00 | 3,432.04 |
| GREYS RIVER | | 927.31 | 0.00 | 0.00 | 0.00 | 0.00 | 0.00 | 0.00 | 0.00 | 927.31 |
| OCEAN LAKE | | 0.00 | 0.00 | 0.00 R | 10,509.14 | 0.00 | 0.00 | 0.00 | 0.00 | 10,509.14 |
| SHERIDAN | | 160.00 | 0.00 | 0.00 | 0.00 | 0.00 | 0.00 | 0.00 | 0.00 | 160.00 |
| SYBILLE | | 681.44 | 0.00 | 0.00 | 0.00 | 0.00 | 0.00 | 0.00 | 0.00 | 681.44 |
| TONGUE RIVER | | 551.05 | 0.00 | 0.00 | 0.00 | 0.00 | 0.00 | 0.00 | 0.00 | 551.05 |
| STATE TOTAL | 6 | 5,751.84 | 0.00 | 0.00 | 10,509.14 | 0.00 | 0.00 | 0.00 | 0.00 | 16,260.98 |
| GRAND TOTAL | 50 | 56,586.61 | 0.00 | 139,273.47 | 55,739.14 | 0.00 | 681.13 | 13,480.00 | 63,564.00 | 315,824.35 |

E - CORPS OF ENGINEERS - DEPARTMENT OF THE ARMY
R - BUREAU OF RECLAMATION - DEPARTMENT OF THE INTERIOR

TABLE 6 - ADMINISTRATIVE SITES

| STATE AND UNIT | RESERVED FROM PUBLIC DOMAIN | | ACQUIRED BY OTHER FEDERAL AGENCY | | DEVISE OR GIFT | PURCHASED | | AGREEMENT EASEMENT OR LEASE | TOTAL ACRES |
| | SOLE OR PRIMARY | SECONDARY | SOLE OR PRIMARY | SECONDARY | | ACRES | COST ($) | | |
|---|---|---|---|---|---|---|---|---|---|
| **ALASKA** | | | | | | | | | |
| BETHEL | 5.08 | 0.00 | 0.00 | 0.00 | 0.00 | 2.08 | 63,600.00 | 0.00 | 7.16 |
| BETTLES | 0.00 | 0.00 | 0.00 | 0.00 | 0.00 | 0.00 | 0.00 | 2.25 | 2.25 |
| COLD BAY HANGAR | 0.00 | 0.00 | 0.00 | 0.00 | 0.00 | 0.00 | 0.00 | 0.39 | 0.39 |
| DILLINGHAM | 0.00 | 0.00 | 0.00 | 0.00 | 0.00 | 11.73 | 488,900.00 | 2.00 | 13.73 |
| EMMONAK | 0.00 | 0.00 | 0.00 | 0.00 | 0.00 | 0.00 | 0.00 | 0.17 | 0.17 |
| FAIRBANKS HANGAR | 0.00 | 0.00 | 0.00 | 0.00 | 0.00 | 0.00 | 0.00 | 2.04 | 2.04 |
| FAIRBANKS OFFICE WILDLIFE | 0.00 | 0.00 | 1.89 | 0.00 | 0.00 | 0.26 | 2,024.05 | 0.00 | 2.15 |
| FORT YUKON | 0.52 | 0.00 | 0.00 | 0.00 | 0.00 | 0.00 | 0.00 | 0.15 | 0.71 |
| GALENA | 0.44 | 0.00 | 0.00 | 0.00 | 0.00 | 2.99 | 50,100.00 | 0.77 | 4.20 |
| HOMER | 0.00 | 0.00 | 0.00 | 0.00 | 0.75 | 50.01 | 1,009,000.00 | 2.00 | 58.76 |
| JUNEAU DOCK | 0.00 | 0.00 | 0.00 | 0.00 | 0.00 | 0.00 | 0.00 | 0.67 | 0.67 |
| JUNEAU HANGAR | 0.00 | 0.00 | 0.00 | 0.00 | 0.00 | 0.00 | 0.00 | 1.06 | 1.06 |
| KAKTOVIK | 0.00 | 0.00 | 0.00 | 0.00 | 0.00 | 0.00 | 0.00 | 0.46 | 0.46 |
| KENAI | 0.00 | 0.00 | 0.00 | 0.00 | 0.00 | 17.68 | 49,500.00 | 0.01 | 17.69 |
| KETCHIKAN | 0.00 | 0.00 | 0.00 | 0.00 | 0.00 | 0.00 | 0.00 | 0.31 | 0.31 |
| KING SALMON | 6.29 | 0.00 | 0.00 | 0.00 | 0.00 | 5.42 | 64,800.00 | 0.34 | 12.05 |
| KODIAK | 2.04 | 0.00 | 0.00 | 2.39 | 0.00 | 0.40 | 715,000.00 | 0.00 | 4.83 |
| KODIAK FLOAT PLANE | 0.00 | 0.00 | 0.00 | 0.00 | 0.00 | 0.00 | 0.00 | 0.06 | 0.06 |
| KODIAK OFFICE | 0.00 CG | 36.00 | 0.00 | 0.00 | 0.00 | 0.00 | 0.00 | 0.00 | 36.00 |
| KOTZEBUE | 0.50 | 0.00 | 0.00 | 0.00 | 0.00 | 0.50 | 209,500.00 | 0.23 | 0.73 |
| KUSTATAN RIVER | 0.00 | 0.00 | 0.00 | 0.00 | 0.00 | 0.00 | 0.00 | 7.00 | 7.00 |
| LAKE HOOD SEAPLANE BASE | 14.90 | 0.00 | 0.00 | 0.00 | 0.00 | 0.00 | 0.00 | 2.26 | 17.16 |
| MCGRATH | 0.00 | 0.00 | 0.00 | 0.00 | 0.00 | 2.44 | 51,000.00 | 0.00 | 2.44 |
| MCLEES LAKE | 0.00 | 0.00 | 0.00 | 0.00 | 0.00 | 0.00 | 0.00 | 0.01 | 0.01 |
| MORTENSENS CREEK | 0.00 | 0.00 | 0.00 | 0.00 | 0.00 | 0.00 | 0.00 | 1.50 | 1.50 |
| PILOT POINT | 1.00 | 0.00 | 0.00 | 0.00 | 0.00 | 0.00 | 0.00 | 0.00 | 1.00 |
| SAINT GEORGE | 0.00 | 0.00 | 0.00 | 0.00 | 0.00 | 0.00 | 0.00 | 1.00 | 1.00 |
| SAINT PAUL | 0.00 | 0.00 | 0.00 | 0.00 | 0.00 | 0.00 | 0.00 | 1.11 | 1.11 |
| SOLDOTNA AIRPORT | 0.00 | 0.00 | 0.00 | 0.00 | 0.00 | 0.00 | 0.00 | 3.92 | 3.92 |
| TOK | 0.00 | 0.00 | 2.00 | 0.00 | 0.00 | 17.88 | 45,000.00 | 0.00 | 19.88 |
| WHITEFISH LAKE | 0.00 | 0.00 | 0.00 | 0.00 | 0.00 | 0.00 | 0.00 | 0.50 | 0.50 |
| STATE TOTAL          31 | 30.27 | 36.00 | 3.89 | 2.39 | 0.75 | 122.39 | 2,758,424.05 | 26.25 | 221.94 |
| **ARIZONA** | | | | | | | | | |
| CABEZA PRIETA | 10.00 | 0.00 | 0.00 | 0.00 | 0.00 | 0.44 | 25,300.00 | 0.00 | 10.44 |
| KOFA | 0.00 | 0.00 | 0.00 | 0.00 | 0.00 | 1.00 | 0.00 | 0.00 | 1.00 |
| STATE TOTAL          2 | 10.00 | 0.00 | 0.00 | 0.00 | 0.00 | 1.44 | 25,300.00 | 0.00 | 11.44 |
| **COLORADO** | | | | | | | | | |
| NAT'L BLACK-FOOTED FERRET | 0.00 | 0.00 | 0.00 | 0.00 | 0.00 | 40.05 | 32,000.00 | 3.89 | 43.94 |
| STATE TOTAL          1 | 0.00 | 0.00 | 0.00 | 0.00 | 0.00 | 40.05 | 32,000.00 | 3.89 | 43.94 |
| **HAWAII** | | | | | | | | | |
| HAWAII | 0.00 | 0.00 | 0.23 | 0.00 | 0.00 | 0.00 | 0.00 | 0.00 | 0.23 |
| MAKENA BEACH | 0.00 | 0.00 | 0.00 | 0.00 | 0.00 | 0.00 | 0.00 | 0.50 | 0.50 |
| OLINDA | 0.00 | 0.00 | 4.20 | 0.00 | 0.00 | 0.00 | 0.00 | 0.00 | 4.20 |
| STATE TOTAL          3 | 0.00 | 0.00 | 4.43 | 0.00 | 0.00 | 0.00 | 0.00 | 0.50 | 4.93 |

TABLE 6 - ADMINISTRATIVE SITES

| STATE AND UNIT | | RESERVED FROM PUBLIC DOMAIN | | ACQUIRED BY OTHER FEDERAL AGENCY | | DEVISE OR GIFT | PURCHASED | | AGREEMENT EASEMENT OR LEASE | TOTAL ACRES |
| | | SOLE OR PRIMARY | SECONDARY | SOLE OR PRIMARY | SECONDARY | | ACRES | COST ($) | | |
|---|---|---|---|---|---|---|---|---|---|---|
| **IOWA** | | | | | | | | | | |
| MCGREGOR | | 0.00 | 0.00 | 0.00 | 0.00 | 0.00 | 4.33 | 155,000.00 | 0.00 | 4.33 |
| STATE TOTAL | 1 | 0.00 | 0.00 | 0.00 | 0.00 | 0.00 | 4.33 | 155,000.00 | 0.00 | 4.33 |
| **KANSAS** | | | | | | | | | | |
| GREAT PLAINS NATURE CTR | | 0.00 | 0.00 | 0.00 | 0.00 | 0.00 | 8.33 | 400,000.00 | 6.22 | 14.55 |
| STATE TOTAL | 1 | 0.00 | 0.00 | 0.00 | 0.00 | 0.00 | 8.33 | 400,000.00 | 6.22 | 14.55 |
| **MICHIGAN** | | | | | | | | | | |
| LAMPREY EEL | | 0.00 | 0.00 | 0.00 | 0.00 | 0.00 | 0.00 | 0.00 | 1.00 | 1.00 |
| STATE TOTAL | 1 | 0.00 | 0.00 | 0.00 | 0.00 | 0.00 | 0.00 | 0.00 | 5.00 | 1.00 |
| **NEW MEXICO** | | | | | | | | | | |
| SAN ANDRES | | 0.00 | 0.00 | 0.00 | 0.00 | 0.00 | 2.16 | 14,000.00 | 0.00 | 2.16 |
| STATE TOTAL | 1 | 0.00 | 0.00 | 0.00 | 0.00 | 0.00 | 2.16 | 14,000.00 | 0.00 | 2.16 |
| **OREGON** | | | | | | | | | | |
| CLARK R. BAVIN | (A) | 0.00 | 0.00 | 0.00 | 0.00 | 0.00 | 0.00 | 0.00 | 4.02 | 4.02 |
| KLAMATH | | 10.04 | 0.00 | 0.00 | 0.00 | 0.00 | 0.00 | 0.00 | 0.00 | 10.04 |
| LAKEVIEW | | 0.00 | 0.00 | 0.25 | 0.00 | 0.00 | 0.00 | 0.00 | 0.00 | 0.25 |
| STATE TOTAL | 3 | 10.04 | 0.00 | 0.25 | 0.00 | 0.00 | 0.00 | 0.00 | 4.02 | 14.31 |
| **WASHINGTON** | | | | | | | | | | |
| MOSES LAKE | | 0.00 | 0.00 | 0.83 | 0.00 | 0.00 | 0.00 | 0.00 | 0.00 | 0.83 |
| STATE TOTAL | 1 | 0.00 | 0.00 | 0.83 | 0.00 | 0.00 | 0.00 | 0.00 | 0.00 | 0.83 |
| **WEST VIRGINIA** | | | | | | | | | | |
| NCTC/TRAINING CENTER | | 0.00 | 0.00 | 0.00 | 0.00 | 0.00 | 860.02 | 7,949,045.00 | 0.00 | 860.02 |
| STATE TOTAL | 1 | 0.00 | 0.00 | 0.00 | 0.00 | 0.00 | 860.02 | 7,949,045.00 | 0.00 | 860.02 |
| GRAND TOTAL | 46 | 50.31 | 36.00 | 9.40 | 2.39 | 0.75 | 1,038.72 | 11,334,769.06 | 41.88 | 1,179.45 |

(A) - FISH AND WILDLIFE FORENSICS LAB
CG - COAST GUARD, DEPARTMENT OF HOMELAND SECURITY
\* - NOT COUNTED

TABLE 7 - NATIONAL FISH HATCHERIES

| STATE AND UNIT | | RESERVED FROM PUBLIC DOMAIN | | ACQUIRED BY OTHER FEDERAL AGENCY | | DEVISE OR GIFT | PURCHASED | | AGREEMENT EASEMENT OR LEASE | TOTAL ACRES |
|---|---|---|---|---|---|---|---|---|---|---|
| | | SOLE OR PRIMARY | SECONDARY | SOLE OR PRIMARY | SECONDARY | | ACRES | COST ($) | | |
| **ARIZONA** | | | | | | | | | | |
| ALCHESAY | | 0.00 | 0.00 | 0.00 | 0.00 | 0.00 | 0.00 | 0.00 | 20.83 | 20.83 |
| WILLIAMS CREEK | | 0.00 | 0.00 | 0.00 | 0.00 | 0.00 | 0.00 | 0.00 | 91.89 | 91.89 |
| WILLOW BEACH | | 0.00 | R 47.81 | 0.00 | 0.00 | 0.00 | 0.00 | 0.00 | 0.00 | 47.81 |
| STATE TOTAL | 3 | 0.00 | 47.81 | 0.00 | 0.00 | 0.00 | 0.00 | 0.00 | 112.72 | 160.53 |
| **ARKANSAS** | | | | | | | | | | |
| GREERS FERRY | | 0.00 | 0.00 | 0.00 | E 31.97 | 0.00 | 0.00 | 0.00 | 0.00 | 31.97 |
| MAMMOTH SPRING | | 0.00 | 0.00 | 0.00 | 0.00 | 0.00 | 36.84 | 55,925.00 | 0.00 | 36.84 |
| NORFORK | | 0.00 | 0.00 | 0.00 | E 46.00 | 0.00 | 0.00 | 0.00 | 0.00 | 46.00 |
| STATE TOTAL | 3 | 0.00 | 0.00 | 0.00 | 77.97 | 0.00 | 36.84 | 55,925.00 | 0.00 | 114.81 |
| **CALIFORNIA** | | | | | | | | | | |
| COLEMAN | | 0.00 | 0.00 | 55.28 | 0.00 | 0.00 | 22.52 | 153,221.00 | 62.97 | 140.77 |
| LIVINGSTON STONE | | 0.00 | 0.00 | 0.00 | 0.00 | 0.00 | 0.00 | 0.00 | 0.40 | 0.40 |
| TEHAMA-COLUSA | (D) | 0.00 | 0.00 | 0.00 | R 350.00 | 0.00 | 0.00 | 0.00 | 0.00 | 350.00 |
| STATE TOTAL | 2 | 0.00 | 0.00 | 55.28 | 350.00 | 0.00 | 22.52 | 153,221.00 | 63.37 | 491.17 |
| **COLORADO** | | | | | | | | | | |
| HOTCHKISS | | 10.00 | 0.00 | 0.00 | 0.00 | 0.00 | 129.17 | 244,776.00 | 2.54 | 141.71 |
| LEADVILLE | | 2,966.34 | 0.00 | 0.00 | 0.00 | 0.00 | 98.79 | 14,400.00 | 0.75 | 3,065.88 |
| STATE TOTAL | 2 | 2,976.34 | 0.00 | 0.00 | 0.00 | 0.00 | 227.96 | 259,176.00 | 3.29 | 3,207.59 |
| **FLORIDA** | | | | | | | | | | |
| WELAKA | | 0.00 | 0.00 | 385.04 | 0.00 | 0.00 | 0.00 | 0.00 | 0.00 | 385.04 |
| STATE TOTAL | 1 | 0.00 | 0.00 | 385.04 | 0.00 | 0.00 | 0.00 | 0.00 | 0.00 | 385.04 |
| **GEORGIA** | | | | | | | | | | |
| BO GINN | (A) | 0.00 | 0.00 | 0.00 | 0.00 | 527.01 | 0.00 | 0.00 | 0.00 | 527.01 |
| CHATTAHOOCHEE FOREST | | 0.00 | 0.00 | 0.00 | F 44.80 | 0.00 | 0.00 | 0.00 | 0.00 | 44.80 |
| WARM SPRINGS | (H) | 0.00 | 0.00 | 0.00 | 0.00 | 18.97 | 39.45 | 110,916.00 | 0.00 | 58.42 |
| STATE TOTAL | 2 | 0.00 | 0.00 | 0.00 | 44.80 | 145.98 | 39.45 | 110,916.00 | 0.00 | 230.23 |
| **IDAHO** | | | | | | | | | | |
| CLEARWATER | (A) | 0.00 | 0.00 | 17.62 | 0.00 | 0.00 | 0.00 | 0.00 | 1.33 | 18.95 |
| DWORSHAK | | 0.00 | 0.00 | 0.00 | E 23.54 | 0.00 | 0.00 | 0.00 | 0.00 | 23.54 |
| EAGLE FISH | (?) | 0.00 | 0.00 | 1.21 | 0.00 | 0.00 | 0.00 | 0.00 | 0.18 | 1.39 |
| HAGERMAN | | 0.00 | 0.00 | 0.00 | 0.00 | 0.00 | 78.79 | 4,566.22 | 0.00 | 78.79 |
| KOOSKIA | | 125.20 | 0.00 | 0.00 | 0.00 | 0.00 | 3.25 | 1.00 | 8.99 | 137.44 |
| MAGIC VALLEY | (A) | 0.00 | 0.00 | 25.46 | 0.00 | 0.00 | 0.00 | 0.00 | 16.98 | 42.44 |
| MCCALL | (A) | 0.00 | 0.00 | 10.91 | 0.00 | 0.00 | 0.00 | 0.00 | 19.05 | 29.96 |
| SAWTOOTH | (A) | 0.00 | 0.00 | 71.66 | 0.00 | 0.00 | 0.00 | 0.00 | 11.63 | 83.29 |
| STATE TOTAL | 3 | 125.20 | 0.00 | 126.86 | 23.54 | 0.00 | 82.04 | 4,567.22 | 58.16 | 415.80 |
| **KENTUCKY** | | | | | | | | | | |
| WOLF CREEK | | 0.00 | 0.00 | 0.00 | E 20.47 | 0.00 | 0.00 | 0.00 | 0.00 | 20.47 |
| STATE TOTAL | 1 | 0.00 | 0.00 | 0.00 | 20.47 | 0.00 | 0.00 | 0.00 | 0.00 | 20.47 |
| **LOUISIANA** | | | | | | | | | | |
| NATCHITOCHES | | 0.00 | 0.00 | 0.00 | 0.00 | 0.00 | 96.99 | 3,954.95 | 0.00 | 96.99 |
| STATE TOTAL | 1 | 0.00 | 0.00 | 0.00 | 0.00 | 0.00 | 96.99 | 3,954.95 | 0.00 | 96.99 |
| **MAINE** | | | | | | | | | | |
| CRAIG BROOK | | 0.00 | 0.00 | 0.00 | 0.00 | 0.00 | 134.65 | 2,000.00 | 0.00 | 134.65 |
| GREEN LAKE | | 0.00 | 0.00 | 0.00 | 0.00 | 0.00 | 128.86 | 32,000.00 | 1.00 | 129.86 |
| STATE TOTAL | 2 | 0.00 | 0.00 | 0.00 | 0.00 | 0.00 | 263.51 | 34,000.00 | 1.00 | 264.51 |
| **MASSACHUSETTS** | | | | | | | | | | |
| BERKSHIRE | (A) | 0.00 | 0.00 | 0.00 | 0.00 | 136.90 | 0.00 | 2,500.00 | 0.00 | 136.90 |
| NORTH ATTLEBORO | | 0.00 | 0.00 | 0.00 | 0.00 | 228.46 | 0.08 | 1,500.00 | 0.00 | 228.54 |
| RICHARD CRONIN | | 0.00 | 0.00 | 0.00 | 0.00 | 58.69 | 0.00 | 0.00 | 0.00 | 58.69 |

TABLE 7 - NATIONAL FISH HATCHERIES

| STATE AND UNIT | | RESERVED FROM PUBLIC DOMAIN | | ACQUIRED BY OTHER FEDERAL AGENCY | | DEVISE OR GIFT | PURCHASED | | AGREEMENT EASEMENT OR LEASE | TOTAL ACRES |
|---|---|---|---|---|---|---|---|---|---|---|
| | | SOLE OR PRIMARY | SECONDARY | SOLE OR PRIMARY | SECONDARY | | ACRES | COST ($) | | |
| **MASSACHUSETTS** | | | | | | | | | | |
| STATE TOTAL | 2 | 0.00 | 0.00 | 0.00 | 0.00 | 425.07 | 0.06 | 4,000.00 | 0.00 | 425.13 |
| **MICHIGAN** | | | | | | | | | | |
| JORDAN RIVER | | 0.00 | 0.00 | 0.00 | 0.00 | 115.84 | 0.00 | 0.00 | 0.00 | 115.84 |
| PENDILLS CREEK | | 0.00 | 0.00 | 0.00 | F 1,648.65 | 0.00 | 84.81 | 4,000.00 | 0.00 | 1,731.48 |
| SULLIVAN CREEK | | 0.00 | 0.00 | 0.00 | F 8.67 | 0.00 | 0.00 | 0.00 | 0.00 | 8.67 |
| STATE TOTAL | 3 | 0.00 | 0.00 | 0.00 | 1,653.32 | 115.84 | 84.81 | 4,000.00 | 0.00 | 1,854.97 |
| **MISSISSIPPI** | | | | | | | | | | |
| MERIDIAN | (A) | 0.00 | 0.00 | 0.00 | 0.00 | 105.86 | 0.00 | 0.00 | 0.00 | 105.86 |
| PRIVATE JOHN ALLEN | | 0.00 | 0.00 | 0.00 | 0.00 | 0.00 | 30.50 | 5,685.00 | 0.00 | 30.50 |
| STATE TOTAL | 1 | 0.00 | 0.00 | 0.00 | 0.00 | 105.86 | 30.50 | 5,685.00 | 0.00 | 136.36 |
| **MISSOURI** | | | | | | | | | | |
| NEOSHO | | 0.00 | 0.00 | 0.00 | 0.00 | 0.30 | 261.33 | 46,027.97 | 11.50 | 273.13 |
| STATE TOTAL | 1 | 0.00 | 0.00 | 0.00 | 0.00 | 0.30 | 261.33 | 46,027.97 | 11.50 | 273.13 |
| **MONTANA** | | | | | | | | | | |
| BOZEMAN | (F) | 0.00 | 0.00 | 0.00 | 0.00 | 42.79 | 130.30 | 4,565.00 | 0.28 | 173.37 |
| CRESTON | | 0.00 | 0.00 | 73.56 | 0.00 | 0.00 | 0.00 | 0.00 | 0.00 | 73.56 |
| ENNIS | | 0.00 | 0.00 | 0.00 | 0.00 | 0.00 | 160.00 | 4,000.00 | 9.32 | 169.32 |
| STATE TOTAL | 2 | 0.00 | 0.00 | 73.56 | 0.00 | 42.79 | 290.30 | 8,565.00 | 9.60 | 416.25 |
| **NEVADA** | | | | | | | | | | |
| AMARGOSA PUPFISH | (D) | 0.00 LM | 159.28 | 0.00 | 0.00 | 0.00 | 0.00 | 0.00 | 0.00 | 159.28 |
| LAHONTAN | | 0.00 | 0.00 | 0.00 | 0.00 | 0.00 | 24.84 | 12,200.00 | 11.06 | 35.90 |
| MARBLE BLUFF | (D) | 0.00 | 0.00 | 0.00 | R 623.20 | 0.00 | 0.00 | 0.00 | 0.00 | 623.20 |
| STATE TOTAL | 1 | 0.00 | 159.28 | 0.00 | 623.20 | 0.00 | 24.84 | 12,200.00 | 11.06 | 818.38 |
| **NEW HAMPSHIRE** | | | | | | | | | | |
| MERRIMACK RIVER | (D) | 0.00 | 0.00 | 0.00 | 0.00 | 0.00 | 8.00 | 24,000.00 | 0.00 | 8.00 |
| NASHUA | | 0.00 | 0.00 | 0.00 | 0.00 | 0.00 | 39.40 | 4,000.00 | 0.00 | 39.40 |
| STATE TOTAL | 1 | 0.00 | 0.00 | 0.00 | 0.00 | 0.00 | 47.40 | 28,000.00 | 0.00 | 47.40 |
| **NEW MEXICO** | | | | | | | | | | |
| DEXTER | (G) | 0.00 | 0.00 | 0.00 | 0.00 | 0.00 | 640.93 | 3,298.90 | 0.00 | 640.93 |
| MORA | (G) | 0.00 | 0.00 | 0.00 | 0.00 | 0.00 | 116.79 | 241,000.00 | 2.00 | 118.79 |
| STATE TOTAL | 2 | 0.00 | 0.00 | 0.00 | 0.00 | 0.00 | 757.72 | 244,298.90 | 2.00 | 759.72 |
| **NORTH CAROLINA** | | | | | | | | | | |
| EDENTON | | 0.00 | 0.00 | 0.00 | 0.00 | 0.00 | 63.59 | 30,000.00 | 0.00 | 63.59 |
| MCKINNEY LAKE | (A) | 0.00 | 0.00 | 408.07 | 0.00 | 0.00 | 14.20 | 72,000.00 | 0.00 | 422.27 |
| STATE TOTAL | 1 | 0.00 | 0.00 | 408.07 | 0.00 | 0.00 | 77.79 | 102,000.00 | 0.00 | 485.86 |
| **NORTH DAKOTA** | | | | | | | | | | |
| BALDHILL DAM | (D) | 0.00 | 0.00 | 0.00 E | 37.10 | 0.00 | 0.00 | 0.00 | 0.00 | 37.10 |
| GARRISON DAM | | 0.00 | 0.00 | 0.00 E | 186.40 | 0.00 | 0.00 | 0.00 | 0.00 | 186.40 |
| VALLEY CITY | | 0.00 | 0.00 | 0.00 | 0.00 | 71.49 | 0.00 | 0.00 | 0.93 | 72.42 |
| STATE TOTAL | 2 | 0.00 | 0.00 | 0.00 | 223.50 | 71.49 | 0.00 | 0.00 | 0.93 | 295.92 |
| **OKLAHOMA** | | | | | | | | | | |
| TISHOMINGO | | 0.00 | 0.00 | 0.00 | 0.00 | 0.00 | 230.95 | 99,137.00 | 3,428.55 | 3,659.50 |
| STATE TOTAL | 1 | 0.00 | 0.00 | 0.00 | 0.00 | 0.00 | 230.95 | 99,137.00 | 3,428.55 | 3,659.50 |
| **OREGON** | | | | | | | | | | |
| EAGLE CREEK | | 40.00 LM | 560.00 | 0.00 | 0.00 | 0.00 | 126.37 | 17,000.00 | 5.40 | 731.77 |
| IRRIGON SATELLITES | (A) | 0.00 | 0.00 | 18.14 | 0.00 | 0.00 | 0.00 | 0.00 | 1.27 | 19.41 |
| LOOKINGGLASS | (A) | 0.00 | 0.00 | 13.49 | 0.00 | 0.00 | 0.00 | 0.00 | 0.00 | 13.49 |
| WARM SPRINGS | | 0.00 | 0.00 | 0.00 | 0.00 | 0.00 | 0.00 | 0.00 | 84.79 | 84.79 |
| STATE TOTAL | 2 | 40.00 | 560.00 | 31.63 | 0.00 | 0.00 | 126.37 | 17,000.00 | 91.46 | 849.46 |

TABLE 7 - NATIONAL FISH HATCHERIES

| STATE AND UNIT | RESERVED FROM PUBLIC DOMAIN | | ACQUIRED BY OTHER FEDERAL AGENCY | | DEVISE OR GIFT | PURCHASED | | AGREEMENT EASEMENT OR LEASE | TOTAL ACRES |
|---|---|---|---|---|---|---|---|---|---|
| | SOLE OR PRIMARY | SECONDARY | SOLE OR PRIMARY | SECONDARY | | ACRES | COST ($) | | |
| **PENNSYLVANIA** | | | | | | | | | |
| ALLEGHENY | 0.00 | 0.00 | 0.00 | E 45.04 | 0.00 | 0.00 | 0.00 | 0.00 | 45.04 |
| LAMAR (H) | 0.00 | 0.00 | 0.00 | 0.00 | 0.00 | 177.21 | 30,552.31 | 0.00 | 177.21 |
| STATE TOTAL 2 | 0.00 | 0.00 | 0.00 | 45.04 | 0.00 | 177.21 | 30,552.31 | 0.00 | 222.25 |
| **SOUTH CAROLINA** | | | | | | | | | |
| BEARS BLUFF | 0.00 | 0.00 | 30.40 | 0.00 | 0.00 | 0.00 | 0.00 | 0.00 | 30.40 |
| ORANGEBURG | 0.00 | 0.00 | 0.00 | 0.00 | 0.00 | 50.65 | 6,573.40 | 0.00 | 50.65 |
| ORANGEBURG COUNTY (D) | 0.00 | 0.00 | 0.00 | 0.00 | 134.01 | 46.65 | 7,500.00 | 0.00 | 180.66 |
| STATE TOTAL 2 | 0.00 | 0.00 | 30.40 | 0.00 | 134.01 | 97.30 | 14,073.40 | 0.00 | 261.71 |
| **SOUTH DAKOTA** | | | | | | | | | |
| D.C. BOOTH (E) | 0.00 | 0.00 | 0.00 | 0.00 | 0.00 | 10.67 | 4,100.00 | 0.12 | 10.79 |
| GAVINS POINT | 0.00 | 0.00 | 0.00 | E 581.00 | 0.00 | 0.00 | 0.00 | 0.00 | 581.00 |
| STATE TOTAL 1 | 0.00 | 0.00 | 0.00 | 581.00 | 0.00 | 10.67 | 4,100.00 | 0.12 | 591.79 |
| **TENNESSEE** | | | | | | | | | |
| DALE HOLLOW | 0.00 | 0.00 | 0.00 | E 40.26 | 0.00 | 0.00 | 0.00 | 0.00 | 40.26 |
| ERWIN | 0.00 | 0.00 | 0.00 | 0.00 | 0.00 | 32.25 | 2,690.34 | 0.00 | 32.25 |
| STATE TOTAL 2 | 0.00 | 0.00 | 0.00 | 40.26 | 0.00 | 32.25 | 2,690.34 | 0.00 | 72.51 |
| **TEXAS** | | | | | | | | | |
| INKS DAM | 0.00 | 0.00 | 0.00 | 0.00 | 94.31 | 0.00 | 0.00 | 79.21 | 173.50 |
| SAN MARCOS (G) | 0.00 | 0.00 | 0.00 | 0.00 | 115.78 | 0.00 | 0.00 | 2.79 | 118.57 |
| UVALDE | 0.00 | 0.00 | 0.00 | 0.00 | 92.00 | 0.00 | 0.00 | 9.00 | 101.00 |
| STATE TOTAL 3 | 0.00 | 0.00 | 0.00 | 0.00 | 302.46 | 0.00 | 0.00 | 91.05 | 393.57 |
| **UTAH** | | | | | | | | | |
| JONES HOLE | 465.55 | 0.00 | 0.00 | 0.00 | 0.00 | 0.00 | 0.00 | 65.50 | 531.05 |
| OURAY (J) | 0.00 | 0.00 | 0.00 | 0.00 | 0.00 | 0.00 | 0.00 | 0.00 | 0.00 |
| STATE TOTAL 2 | 465.55 | 0.00 | 0.00 | 0.00 | 0.00 | 0.00 | 0.00 | 65.50 | 531.05 |
| **VERMONT** | | | | | | | | | |
| PITTSFORD | 0.00 | 0.00 | 0.00 | 0.00 | 0.00 | 35.09 | 13,010.00 | 0.00 | 35.09 |
| WHITE RIVER | 0.00 | 0.00 | 0.00 | 0.00 | 0.00 | 53.50 | 133,320.00 | 15.00 | 68.50 |
| STATE TOTAL 2 | 0.00 | 0.00 | 0.00 | 0.00 | 0.00 | 88.59 | 146,330.00 | 15.00 | 103.59 |
| **VIRGINIA** | | | | | | | | | |
| HARRISON LAKE | 0.00 | 0.00 | 0.00 | 0.00 | 0.00 | 444.73 | 116,988.50 | 0.00 | 444.73 |
| PAINT BANK (A) | 0.00 | 0.00 | 0.00 | 0.00 | 0.00 | 0.00 | 51,500.00 | 0.00 | 0.00 |
| WYTHEVILLE (A) | 0.00 | 0.00 | 0.00 | 0.00 | 0.00 | 0.00 | 52,000.00 | 0.00 | 0.00 |
| STATE TOTAL 1 | 0.00 | 0.00 | 0.00 | 0.00 | 0.00 | 444.73 | 219,988.50 | 0.00 | 444.73 |
| **WASHINGTON** | | | | | | | | | |
| ABERNATHY (C) | 0.00 | 0.00 | 0.00 | 0.00 | 0.00 | 98.52 | 10,789.00 | 3.10 | 101.62 |
| CARSON | 0.00 | F 220.00 | 0.00 | 0.00 | 0.00 | 0.00 | 0.00 | 0.00 | 220.00 |
| ENTIAT | 0.00 | 0.00 | 34.27 | 0.00 | 0.00 | 0.00 | 0.00 | 0.08 | 34.35 |
| LEAVENWORTH | 0.00 | 0.00 | 861.15 | 0.00 | 11.40 | 4.07 | 84,000.00 | 0.43 | 877.05 |
| LITTLE WHITE SALMON | 0.00 | 0.00 | 211.39 | 0.00 | 1.34 | 202.44 | 476,378.00 | 16.10 | 431.27 |
| LYONS FERRY (A) | 0.00 | 0.00 | 110.25 | 0.00 | 0.00 | 0.00 | 0.00 | 28.65 | 138.89 |
| MAKAH | 0.00 | 0.00 | 0.00 | 0.00 | 0.00 | 0.00 | 0.00 | 81.85 | 81.85 |
| NISQUALLY (B) | 0.00 | 0.00 | 0.00 | 0.00 | 0.00 | 0.00 | 0.00 | 155.81 | 155.81 |
| QUILCENE | 0.00 | 0.00 | 0.00 | 0.00 | 3.28 | 31.50 | 466,500.00 | 12.52 | 47.40 |
| QUINAULT | 0.00 | 0.00 | 81.37 | 0.00 | 0.00 | 0.00 | 6,550.00 | 15.06 | 96.43 |
| SPRING CREEK | 0.00 | 0.00 | 0.00 | E 24.20 | 0.00 | 55.70 | 87,475.00 | 9.67 | 89.57 |
| TUCANNON (A) | 0.00 | 0.00 | 16.82 | 0.00 | 0.00 | 0.00 | 0.00 | 32.10 | 48.92 |
| WILLARD | 0.00 | 0.00 | 0.00 | 0.00 | 0.00 | 10.10 | 6,750.00 | 3.70 | 83.80 |
| WINTHROP | 0.00 | 0.00 | 41.56 | 0.00 | 0.00 | 0.00 | 0.00 | 12.37 | 52.90 |
| STATE TOTAL 10 | 0.00 | 220.00 | 1,356.84 | 24.20 | 16.12 | 472.83 | 1,128,372.00 | 371.40 | 2,460.89 |
| **WEST VIRGINIA** | | | | | | | | | |

TABLE 7 - NATIONAL FISH HATCHERIES

| STATE AND UNIT | RESERVED FROM PUBLIC DOMAIN | | ACQUIRED BY OTHER FEDERAL AGENCY | | DEVISE OR GIFT | PURCHASED | | AGREEMENT EASEMENT OR LEASE | TOTAL ACRES |
|---|---|---|---|---|---|---|---|---|---|
| | SOLE OR PRIMARY | SECONDARY | SOLE OR PRIMARY | SECONDARY | | ACRES | COST ($) | | |
| **WEST VIRGINIA** | | | | | | | | | |
| WHITE SULPHUR SPRINGS | 0.00 | 0.00 | 0.00 | 0.00 | 0.00 | 60.04 | 79,500.00 | 0.70 | 60.74 |
| STATE TOTAL 1 | 0.00 | 0.00 | 0.00 | 0.00 | 0.00 | 60.04 | 79,500.00 | 0.70 | 60.74 |
| **WISCONSIN** | | | | | | | | | |
| GENOA (1) | 0.00 | 0.00 | 0.00 | 0.00 | 0.00 | 0.00 | 0.00 | 0.00 | 0.00 |
| IRON RIVER | 0.00 | 0.00 | 0.00 | 0.00 | 0.00 | 1,200.83 | 525,490.00 | 0.00 | 1,200.83 |
| STATE TOTAL 2 | 0.00 | 0.00 | 0.00 | 0.00 | 0.00 | 1,200.83 | 525,490.00 | 0.00 | 1,200.83 |
| **WYOMING** | | | | | | | | | |
| JACKSON (2) | 0.00 | 0.00 | 0.00 | 0.00 | 0.00 | 0.00 | 0.00 | 0.00 | 0.00 |
| SARATOGA | 0.00 | 0.00 | 0.00 | 0.00 | 0.00 | 118.73 | 174,800.00 | 1.21 | 119.94 |
| STATE TOTAL 2 | 0.00 | 0.00 | 0.00 | 0.00 | 0.00 | 118.73 | 174,800.00 | 1.21 | 119.94 |
| GRAND TOTAL 69 | 3,607.09 | 987.09 | 2,467.68 | 3,707.30 | 1,358.94 | 5,406.06 | 3,518,403.59 | 4,541.42 | 21,873.58 |

(A) - HATCHERY MANAGED/OPERATED BY STATE
(B) - HATCHERY MANAGED/OPERATED BY TRIBE
(C) - FISH TECHNOLOGY CENTER
(D) - OTHER NON-NATIONAL FISH HATCHERY OR FISHERIES FACILITY
(E) - HISTORIC NATIONAL FISH HATCHERY
(F) - FISH TECHNOLOGY CENTER AND FISH HEALTH CENTER
(G) - NATIONAL FISH HATCHERY AND FISH TECHNOLOGY CENTER
(H) - NATIONAL FISH HATCHERY, FISH TECHNOLOGY CENTER AND FISH HEALTH CENTER
(I) - FISH HEALTH LAB MANAGED/OPERATED BY STATE

(1) - LOCATED ON THE UPPER MISSISSIPPI REFUGE
(2) - LOCATED ON THE NATIONAL ELK REFUGE
(3) - LOCATED ON THE OURAY NATIONAL WILDLIFE REFUGE

E  - CORPS OF ENGINEERS, DEPARTMENT OF THE ARMY
F  - FOREST SERVICE, DEPARTMENT OF AGRICULTURE
LM - BUREAU OF LAND MANAGEMENT, DEPARTMENT OF THE INTERIOR
R  - BUREAU OF RECLAMATION, DEPARTMENT OF THE INTERIOR

*  - NOT COUNTED AS A NATIONAL FISH HATCHERY

| STATE AND UNIT | WILDERNESS NAME | WILDERNESS ACRES | REFUGE ACRES | PUBLIC LAW | |
|---|---|---|---|---|---|
| | | | | NUMBER | DATE |
| ALASKA | | | | | |
| ALASKA MARITIME | ALEUTIAN ISLANDS | 1,300,000.00 | 3,417,756.91 | 96-487 | 12/02/80 |
| ALASKA MARITIME | BERING SEA | 81,340.00 | 0.00 | 91-504 | 10/23/70 |
| ALASKA MARITIME | BOGOSLOF | 175.00 | 0.00 | 91-504 | 10/23/70 |
| ALASKA MARITIME | CHAMISSO | 455.00 | 0.00 | 93-632 | 01/03/75 |
| ALASKA MARITIME | FORRESTER ISLAND | 2,832.00 | 0.00 | 91-504 | 10/23/70 |
| ALASKA MARITIME | HAZY ISLAND | 32.00 | 0.00 | 91-504 | 10/23/70 |
| ALASKA MARITIME | SEMIDI | 250,000.00 | 0.00 | 96-487 | 12/02/80 |
| ALASKA MARITIME | SIMEONOF | 25,855.00 | 0.00 | 94-557 | 10/19/76 |
| ALASKA MARITIME | ST. LAZARIA | 65.00 | 0.00 | 91-504 | 10/23/70 |
| ALASKA MARITIME | TUXEDNI | 5,566.00 | 0.00 | 91-504 | 10/23/70 |
| ALASKA MARITIME | UNIMAK | 910,000.00 | 0.00 | 96-487 | 12/02/80 |
| ARCTIC | MOLLIE BEATTIE | 8,000,000.00 | 19,286,322.34 | 96-487 | 12/02/80 |
| BECHAROF | BECHAROF | 400,000.00 | 1,200,060.27 | 96-487 | 12/02/80 |
| INNOKO | INNOKO | 1,240,000.00 | 3,850,481.05 | 96-487 | 12/02/80 |
| IZEMBEK | IZEMBEK | 307,981.76 | 311,075.78 | 96-487 | 12/02/80 |
| KENAI | KENAI | 1,354,247.00 | 1,912,425.40 | 96-487 | 12/02/80 |
| KOYUKUK | KOYUKUK | 400,000.00 | 3,550,160.27 | 96-487 | 12/02/80 |
| SELAWIK | SELAWIK | 240,000.00 | 2,150,161.99 | 96-487 | 12/02/80 |
| TOGIAK | TOGIAK | 2,272,946.51 | 4,101,177.63 | 96-487 | 12/02/80 |
| YUKON DELTA | ANDREAFSKY | 1,300,000.00 | 19,162,296.50 | 96-487 | 12/02/80 |
| | NUNIVAK | 600,000.00 | | 96-487 | 12/02/80 |
| STATE TOTAL | | 18,691,495.27 | 58,941,918.14 | | |
| ARIZONA | | | | | |
| CABEZA PRIETA | CABEZA PRIETA | 803,418.00 | 860,041.32 | 101-628 | 11/28/90 |
| HAVASU | HAVASU | 14,606.00 | 30,273.82 | 101-628 | 11/28/90 |
| IMPERIAL | IMPERIAL REFUGE WILDERNESS | 9,220.00 | 17,809.76 | 101-628 | 11/28/90 |
| KOFA | KOFA | 516,200.00 | 666,480.00 | 101-628 | 11/28/90 |
| STATE TOTAL | | 1,343,444.00 | 1,574,610.90 | | |
| ARKANSAS | | | | | |
| BIG LAKE | BIG LAKE | 2,143.80 | 11,036.10 | 94-557 | 10/19/76 |
| STATE TOTAL | | 2,143.80 | 11,036.10 | | |
| CALIFORNIA | | | | | |
| FARALLON | FARALLON | 141.00 | 211.00 | 93-550 | 12/26/74 |
| HAVASU | HAVASU | 3,195.00 | 7,235.34 | 103-433 | 10/31/94 |
| IMPERIAL | IMPERIAL | 5,836.00 | 7,958.19 | 103-433 | 10/31/94 |
| STATE TOTAL | | 9,172.00 | 15,404.53 | | |
| COLORADO | | | | | |
| LEADVILLE* | MOUNT MASSIVE | 2,560.00 | 3,065.88 | 96-560 | 12/22/80 |
| STATE TOTAL | | 2,560.00 | 3,065.88 | | |
| FLORIDA | | | | | |
| CEDAR KEYS | CEDAR KEYS | 379.00 | 891.15 | 92-364 | 08/07/72 |
| CHASSAHOWITZKA | CHASSAHOWITZKA | 23,578.93 | 30,842.91 | 94-557 | 10/19/76 |
| GREAT WHITE HERON | FLORIDA KEYS | 1,900.00 | 117,683.13 | 93-632 | 01/03/75 |
| ISLAND BAY | ISLAND BAY | 20.24 | 20.24 | 91-504 | 10/23/70 |
| J.N. "DING" DARLING | J.N. "DING" DARLING | 2,619.13 | 6,406.79 | 94-557 | 10/19/76 |
| KEY WEST | FLORIDA KEYS | 2,019.00 | 208,308.17 | 93-632 | 01/03/75 |
| LAKE WOODRUFF | LAKE WOODRUFF | 1,066.00 | 21,559.02 | 94-557 | 10/19/76 |
| NATIONAL KEY DEER | FLORIDA KEYS(1) | 2,278.00 | 84,096.54 | 93-632 | 01/03/75 |
| PASSAGE KEY | PASSAGE KEY | 36.37 | 63.87 | 91-504 | 10/23/70 |
| PELICAN ISLAND | PELICAN ISLAND | 5.50 | 5,410.44 | 91-504 | 10/23/70 |
| ST. MARKS | ST. MARKS | 17,350.00 | 69,196.75 | 93-632 | 01/03/75 |
| STATE TOTAL | | 51,252.17 | 544,479.01 | | |

| STATE AND UNIT | WILDERNESS NAME | WILDERNESS ACRES | REFUGE ACRES | PUBLIC LAW NUMBER | PUBLIC LAW DATE |
|---|---|---|---|---|---|
| GEORGIA | | | | | |
| BLACKBEARD ISLAND | BLACKBEARD ISLAND | 3,000.00 | 5,617.64 | 93-632 | 10/23/70 |
| OKEFENOKEE | OKEFENOKEE | 353,981.00 | 398,183.90 | 93-429 | 10/01/74 |
| WOLF ISLAND | WOLF ISLAND | 5,125.82 | 5,125.82 | 93-632 | 01/03/75 |
| STATE TOTAL | | 362,106.82 | 408,927.36 | | |
| ILLINOIS | | | | | |
| CRAB ORCHARD | CRAB ORCHARD | 4,050.00 | 43,909.42 | 94-557 | 10/19/76 |
| STATE TOTAL | | 4,050.00 | 43,909.42 | | |
| LOUISIANA | | | | | |
| BRETON | BRETON | 5,000.00 | 9,047.00 | 93-632 | 01/01/75 |
| LACASSINE | LACASSINE | 3,345.60 | 34,378.77 | 94-557 | 10/19/76 |
| STATE TOTAL | | 8,345.60 | 43,425.77 | | |
| MAINE | | | | | |
| MOOSEHORN | BARING UNIT | 4,680.00 | 28,874.66 | 93-632 | 01/03/75 |
| | BIRCH ISLANDS UNIT | 6.00 | | 91-504 | 10/23/70 |
| | EDMUNDS UNIT | 2,706.00 | | 91-504 | 10/23/70 |
| STATE TOTAL | | 7,392.00 | 28,874.66 | | |
| MASSACHUSETTS | | | | | |
| MONOMOY | MONOMOY | 3,244.00 | 7604.00 | 91-504 | 10/23/70 |
| STATE TOTAL | | 3,244.00 | 7,604.00 | | |
| MICHIGAN | | | | | |
| HURON | HURON ISLANDS | 147.50 | 146.85 | 91-504 | 10/23/70 |
| MICHIGAN ISLANDS | MICHIGAN ISLANDS | 12.00 | 597.39 | 91-504 | 10/23/70 |
| SENEY | SENEY | 25,150.00 | 95,244.81 | 91-504 | 10/23/70 |
| STATE TOTAL | | 25,309.50 | 95,989.05 | | |
| MINNESOTA | | | | | |
| AGASSIZ | AGASSIZ | 4,000.00 | 61,500.93 | 94-557 | 10/19/76 |
| TAMARAC | TAMARAC | 2,180.00 | 35,191.38 | 94-557 | 10/19/76 |
| STATE TOTAL | | 6,180.00 | 96,692.31 | | |
| MISSOURI | | | | | |
| MINGO | MINGO | 7,730.00 | 21,661.05 | 94-557 | 10/19/76 |
| STATE TOTAL | | 7,730.00 | 21,661.05 | | |
| MONTANA | | | | | |
| MEDICINE LAKE | MEDICINE LAKE | 11,366.00 | 31,533.71 | 94-557 | 10/19/76 |
| RED ROCK LAKES | RED ROCK LAKES | 32,350.00 | 68,810.25 | 94-557 | 10/19/76 |
| UL BEND | UL BEND | 20,819.00 | 56,049.56 | 94-557 | 10/19/76 |
| | | | | 98-140 | 10/31/83 |
| STATE TOTAL | | 64,535.00 | 156,393.52 | | |
| NEBRASKA | | | | | |
| FORT NIOBRARA | FORT NIOBRARA | 4,635.00 | 19,132.53 | 94-557 | 10/19/76 |
| STATE TOTAL | | 4,635.00 | 19,132.53 | | |
| NEW JERSEY | | | | | |
| EDWIN B. FORSYTHE | BRIGANTINE | 6,681.00 | 46,489.50 | 93-632 | 01/03/75 |
| GREAT SWAMP | GREAT SWAMP | 3,660.00 | 7,657.45 | 90-532 | 09/28/68 |
| STATE TOTAL | | 10,341.00 | 54,146.95 | | |
| NEW MEXICO | | | | | |
| BITTER LAKE | SALT CREEK | 9,621.00 | 24,608.64 | 91-504 | 10/23/70 |
| BOSQUE DEL APACHE | CHUPADEA WILDERNESS AREA | 5,289.00 | 57,191.10 | 93-632 | 01/03/75 |
| | INDIAN WELL WILDERNESS AREA | 5,139.00 | | 93-632 | 01/03/75 |
| | LITTLE SAN PASCUAL WILDERNESS | 19,859.00 | | 93-632 | 01/03/75 |
| STATE TOTAL | | 39,908.00 | 81,799.74 | | |

| STATE AND UNIT | WILDERNESS NAME | WILDERNESS ACRES | REFUGE ACRES | PUBLIC LAW NUMBER | PUBLIC LAW DATE |
|---|---|---|---|---|---|
| NORTH CAROLINA | | | | | |
| SWANQUARTER | SWANQUARTER | 8,784.93 | 16,411.09 | 94-557 | 10/19/76 |
| STATE TOTAL | | 8,784.93 | 16,411.09 | | |
| NORTH DAKOTA | | | | | |
| CHASE LAKE | CHASE LAKE | 4,155.00 | 4,449.47 | 93-632 | 01/03/75 |
| LOSTWOOD | LOSTWOOD | 5,577.00 | 26,903.99 | 93-632 | 01/03/75 |
| STATE TOTAL | | 9,732.00 | 31,353.46 | | |
| OHIO | | | | | |
| WEST SISTER ISLAND | WEST SISTER ISLAND | 77.00 | 80.13 | 93-632 | 01/03/75 |
| STATE TOTAL | | 77.00 | 80.13 | | |
| OKLAHOMA | | | | | |
| WICHITA MOUNTAINS | CHARONS GARDEN UNIT | 5,723.00 | 59,019.60 | 91-504 | 10/23/70 |
| | NORTH MOUNTAIN UNIT | 2,847.00 | | 91-504 | 10/23/70 |
| STATE TOTAL | | 8,570.00 | 59,019.60 | | |
| OREGON | | | | | |
| OREGON ISLANDS | OREGON ISLANDS | 925.06 | 1,079.61 | 91-504 | 10/23/70 |
| THREE ARCH ROCKS | THREE ARCH ROCKS | 15.00 | 15.00 | 91-504 | 10/23/70 |
| STATE TOTAL | | 940.06 | 1,094.61 | | |
| SOUTH CAROLINA | | | | | |
| CAPE ROMAIN | CAPE ROMAIN | 29,000.00 | 66,287.18 | 93-632 | 01/03/75 |
| STATE TOTAL | | 29,000.00 | 66,287.18 | | |
| WASHINGTON | | | | | |
| COPALIS | WASHINGTON ISLANDS | 60.80 | 60.80 | 91-504 | 10/23/70 |
| FLATTERY ROCKS | WASHINGTON ISLANDS | 125.00 | 125.00 | 91-504 | 10/23/70 |
| QUILLAYUTE NEEDLES | WASHINGTON ISLANDS | 300.20 | 300.20 | 91-504 | 10/23/70 |
| SAN JUAN ISLANDS | SAN JUAN ISLANDS | 353.00 | 448.53 | 94-557 | 10/19/76 |
| STATE TOTAL | | 839.00 | 934.53 | | |
| WISCONSIN | | | | | |
| GRAVEL ISLAND | WISCONSIN ISLANDS | 27.00 | 27.00 | 91-504 | 10/23/70 |
| GREEN BAY | WISCONSIN ISLANDS | 2.00 | 2.00 | 91-504 | 10/23/70 |
| STATE TOTAL | | 29.00 | 29.00 | | |
| GRAND TOTAL | | 20,701,816.15 | 62,324,280.57 | | |

*Located on the Leadville National Fish Hatchery

| STATE AND UNIT | ACRES UNDER PRIMARY CONTROL OF | | | | TOTAL ACRES |
| --- | --- | --- | --- | --- | --- |
| | CORPS OF ENGINEERS | BUREAU OF RECLAMATION | TENNESSEE VALLEY AUTHORITY | FISH AND WILDLIFE SERVICE | |
| ALABAMA | | | | | |
| CHOCTAW | 4,218.00 | 0.00 | 0.00 | 0.00 | 4,218.00 |
| EUFAULA | 7,929.00 | 0.00 | 0.00 | 24.19 | 7,953.19 |
| WHEELER | 0.00 | 0.00 | 25,674.62 | 8,756.04 | 34,430.66 |
| STATE TOTAL | 12,147.00 | 0.00 | 25,674.62 | 9,213.29 | 46,601.85 |
| ARIZONA | | | | | |
| BILL WILLIAMS | 0.00 | 1699.07 | 0.00 | 4,355.69 | 6,054.76 |
| CIBOLA | 0.00 | 623.38 | 0.00 | 7,982.66 | 8,606.04 |
| HAVASU | 0.00 | 20,235.28 | 0.00 | 10,044.54 | 30,279.82 |
| IMPERIAL | 0.00 | 17,166.14 | 0.00 | 643.62 | 17,809.76 |
| STATE TOTAL | 0.00 | 39,723.87 | 0.00 | 23,026.51 | 62,750.38 |
| ARKANSAS | | | | | |
| POND CREEK | 700.00 | 0.00 | 0.00 | 26,529.43 | 27,229.43 |
| WHITE RIVER | 45.80 | 0.00 | 0.00 | 158,290.80 | 158,336.60 |
| STATE TOTAL | 745.80 | 0.00 | 0.00 | 184,820.23 | 185,566.03 |
| CALIFORNIA | | | | | |
| CLEAR LAKE | 0.00 | 11,103.43 | 0.00 | 13,020.07 | 24,123.50 |
| HAVASU | 0.00 | 7,225.34 | 0.00 | 10.00 | 7,235.34 |
| IMPERIAL | 0.00 | 7,958.19 | 0.00 | 0.00 | 7,958.19 |
| SONNY BONO SALTON SEA | 0.00 | 23,424.58 | 0.00 | 14,234.29 | 37,658.87 |
| STATE TOTAL | 0.00 | 49,711.54 | 0.00 | 27,264.36 | 76,975.90 |
| GEORGIA | | | | | |
| EUFAULA | 3,231.00 | 0.00 | 0.00 | 0.00 | 3,231.00 |
| STATE TOTAL | 3,231.00 | 0.00 | 0.00 | 0.00 | 3,231.00 |
| IDAHO | | | | | |
| DEER FLAT | 0.00 | 9,993.28 | 0.00 | 554.29 | 10,547.57 |
| MINIDOKA | 0.00 | 17,923.12 | 0.00 | 2,828.64 | 20,751.76 |
| STATE TOTAL | 0.00 | 27,916.40 | 0.00 | 3,382.93 | 31,299.33 |
| ILLINOIS | | | | | |
| GREAT RIVER | 5,490.81 | 0.00 | 0.00 | 1,619.82 | 7,110.63 |
| PORT LOUISA | 1,466.00 | 0.00 | 0.00 | 4.89 | 1,470.89 |
| TWO RIVERS | 7,017.00 | 0.00 | 0.00 | 1,016.20 | 8,033.20 |
| UPPER MISSISSIPPI RIVER | 26,956.47 | 0.00 | 0.00 | 6,334.70 | 33,291.17 |
| STATE TOTAL | 40,930.28 | 0.00 | 0.00 | 8,975.61 | 49,905.89 |
| IOWA | | | | | |
| PORT LOUISA | 10,423.94 | 0.00 | 0.00 | 12,199.44 | 22,623.38 |
| UPPER MISSISSIPPI RIVER | 30,315.00 | 0.00 | 0.00 | 20,832.78 | 51,147.78 |
| STATE TOTAL | 40,738.94 | 0.00 | 0.00 | 33,032.22 | 73,771.16 |
| KANSAS | | | | | |
| FLINT HILLS | 18,463.21 | 0.00 | 0.00 | 0.15 | 18,463.36 |
| KIRWIN | 0.00 | 10,778.00 | 0.00 | 0.00 | 10,778.00 |
| STATE TOTAL | 18,463.21 | 10,778.00 | 0.00 | 0.15 | 29,241.36 |
| LOUISIANA | | | | | |
| DELTA | 2,892.30 | 0.00 | 0.00 | 45,906.80 | 48,799.10 |
| STATE TOTAL | 2,892.30 | 0.00 | 0.00 | 45,906.80 | 48,799.10 |
| MINNESOTA | | | | | |
| BIG STONE | 254.20 | 0.00 | 0.00 | 11,331.22 | 11,585.42 |
| UPPER MISSISSIPPI RIVER | 15,420.77 | 0.00 | 0.00 | 18,360.46 | 33,781.23 |
| STATE TOTAL | 15,674.97 | 0.00 | 0.00 | 29,691.68 | 45,366.65 |
| MISSISSIPPI | | | | | |
| PANTHER SWAMP | 7,070.45 | 0.00 | 0.00 | 28,890.80 | 35,961.25 |
| STATE TOTAL | 7,070.45 | 0.00 | 0.00 | 28,890.80 | 35,961.25 |

| STATE AND UNIT | ACRES UNDER PRIMARY CONTROL OF | | | | TOTAL ACRES |
| | CORPS OF ENGINEERS | BUREAU OF RECLAMATION | TENNESSEE VALLEY AUTHORITY | FISH AND WILDLIFE SERVICE | |
|---|---|---|---|---|---|
| MISSOURI | | | | | |
| TWO RIVERS | 232.00 | 0.00 | 0.00 | 0.00 | 232.00 |
| STATE TOTAL | 232.00 | 0.00 | 0.00 | 0.00 | 232.00 |
| MONTANA | | | | | |
| CHARLES M. RUSSELL | 528,300.14 | 0.00 | 0.00 | 386,964.08 | 915,264.22 |
| UL BEND | 14,823.36 | 0.00 | 0.00 | 41,226.20 | 56,049.56 |
| STATE TOTAL | 543,123.50 | 0.00 | 0.00 | 428,190.28 | 971,313.78 |
| NEBRASKA | | | | | |
| NORTH PLATTE | 0.00 | 2,684.81 | 0.00 | 788.42 | 3,473.23 |
| STATE TOTAL | 0.00 | 2,684.81 | 0.00 | 788.42 | 3,473.23 |
| NEVADA | | | | | |
| FALLON | 0.00 | 17,901.94 | 0.00 | 0.00 | 17,901.94 |
| STATE TOTAL | 0.00 | 17,901.94 | 0.00 | 0.00 | 17,901.94 |
| NEW MEXICO | | | | | |
| MAXWELL | 0.00 | 438.52 | 0.00 | 3,260.07 | 3,698.59 |
| STATE TOTAL | 0.00 | 438.52 | 0.00 | 3,260.07 | 3,698.59 |
| NORTH DAKOTA | | | | | |
| AUDUBON | 14,739.19 | 0.00 | 0.00 | 0.00 | 14,739.19 |
| STATE TOTAL | 14,739.19 | 0.00 | 0.00 | 0.00 | 14,739.19 |
| OKLAHOMA | | | | | |
| OPTIMA | 4,332.81 | 0.00 | 0.00 | 0.00 | 4,332.81 |
| SALT PLAINS | 11,565.28 | 0.00 | 0.00 | 20,491.84 | 32,057.12 |
| SEQUOYAH | 20,800.00 | 0.00 | 0.00 | 0.00 | 20,800.00 |
| TISHOMINGO | 16,464.18 | 0.00 | 0.00 | 0.00 | 16,464.18 |
| WASHITA | 0.00 | 8,061.81 | 0.00 | 13.56 | 8,075.37 |
| STATE TOTAL | 53,162.27 | 8,061.81 | 0.00 | 20,505.40 | 81,729.48 |
| OREGON | | | | | |
| COLD SPRINGS | 0.00 | 2,679.95 | 0.00 | 436.88 | 3,116.83 |
| MCKAY CREEK | 0.00 | 1,813.00 | 0.00 | 23.50 | 1,836.50 |
| UMATILLA | 7,430.37 | 0.00 | 0.00 | 1,477.00 | 8,907.37 |
| STATE TOTAL | 7,430.37 | 4,492.95 | 0.00 | 1,937.38 | 13,860.70 |
| SOUTH CAROLINA | | | | | |
| TYBEE | 100.00 | 0.00 | 0.00 | 0.00 | 100.00 |
| STATE TOTAL | 100.00 | 0.00 | 0.00 | 0.00 | 100.00 |
| TENNESSEE | | | | | |
| CROSS CREEKS | 2,442.00 | 0.00 | 0.00 | 6,419.49 | 8,861.49 |
| TENNESSEE | 0.00 | 0.00 | 50,830.30 | 529.16 | 51,359.46 |
| STATE TOTAL | 2,442.00 | 0.00 | 50,830.30 | 6,948.65 | 60,220.95 |
| TEXAS | | | | | |
| HAGERMAN | 11,319.84 | 0.00 | 0.00 | 0.00 | 11,319.84 |
| STATE TOTAL | 11,319.84 | 0.00 | 0.00 | 0.00 | 11,319.84 |
| WASHINGTON | | | | | |
| COLUMBIA | 0.00 | 2,662.00 | 0.00 | 26,934.27 | 29,596.27 |
| MCNARY | 11,895.00 | 0.00 | 0.00 | 3,610.39 | 15,505.39 |
| UMATILLA | 13,209.50 | 0.00 | 0.00 | 1,666.33 | 14,875.83 |
| STATE TOTAL | 25,104.50 | 2,662.00 | 0.00 | 32,210.99 | 59,977.49 |
| WISCONSIN | | | | | |
| UPPER MISSISSIPPI RIVER | 40,341.00 | 0.00 | 0.00 | 49,270.24 | 89,611.24 |
| STATE TOTAL | 40,341.00 | 0.00 | 0.00 | 49,270.24 | 89,611.24 |
| WYOMING | | | | | |
| PATHFINDER | 0.00 | 14,512.06 | 0.00 | 2,294.84 | 16,806.90 |
| STATE TOTAL | 0.00 | 14,512.06 | 0.00 | 2,294.84 | 16,806.90 |
| GRAND TOTAL | 839,888.62 | 178,883.90 | 76,504.92 | 939,610.85 | 2,034,455.23 |

# Notes

In addition to the changes noted in the accomplishments section and those noted below, the figures in our tables may show some changes from previous annual reports. For example, decreases in acreage figures may reflect expired leases, real property disposals made in land exchanges, or property transfers. You may notice an increase or decrease after we complete new property surveys or when we enter additional information into the database after the Regions transmit the data for publication. Other changes result from corrections made when we found errors in the historical data previously entered into the database systems or when we had not previously entered information into the database.

**Table 2A:** Negative acreage will appear in Table 2A when we dispose of or transfer more acres than we acquire during the fiscal year.

**Table 3:** We established two additional refuges: Neches River NWR in Texas and Rocky Mountain Front Conservation Area in Montana (see Accomplishments section of this report.)

**Tables 3 and 4:** The report summarizes Farm Service Agency (formerly Farmers Home Administration), Department of Agriculture, units in Table 3 by state and in Table 4 by state and county. These entries, identified as "AFSA Interest" consist of lands or interests in lands acquired from the Farm Service Agency that are not located within existing project boundaries. We include FSA units in state and county acreage totals but do not count them as separate units.

**Table 4:** The Waterfowl Production Areas are units of the National Wildlife Refuge System established under the Migratory Bird Hunting and Conservation Stamp Act. For purposes of this report, we roll up the acreage of the WPAs by county in each state, and we show the total number of NWRS Waterfowl Production Area units as the total number of approved counties with WPA acres.

**Table 7:** We count the Ouray hatchery in Utah as a National Fish Hatchery; but it is located on the Ouray National Wildlife Refuge, and we include the acreage in Table 3 rather than Table 7. The Service manages the Hagerman National Fish Hatchery in Idaho, but the State manages remainder of the land and appears in Table 5 as the Hagerman Coordination Area.